METROPOLITAN
ANTHONY
OF SOUROZH

MODERN SPIRITUAL MASTERS
Robert Ellsberg, Series Editor

This series introduces the writing and vision of some of the great spiritual masters of the twentieth century. Along with selections from their writings, each volume includes a comprehensive introduction, presenting the author's life and writings in context and drawing attention to points of special relevance to contemporary spirituality.

Some of these authors found a wide audience in their lifetimes. In other cases recognition has come long after their deaths. Some are rooted in long-established traditions of spirituality. Others charted new, untested paths. In each case, however, the authors in this series have engaged in a spiritual journey shaped by the influences and concerns of our age. Such concerns include the challenges of modern science, religious pluralism, secularism, and the quest for social justice.

At the dawn of a new millennium this series commends these modern spiritual masters, along with the saints and witnesses of previous centuries, as guides and companions to a new generation of seekers.

MODERN SPIRITUAL MASTERS SERIES

METROPOLITAN ANTHONY OF SOUROZH

Essential Writings

Selected with an Introduction by

GILLIAN CROW

Maryknoll, New York 10545

Founded in 1970, Orbis Books endeavors to publish works that enlighten the mind, nourish the spirit, and challenge the conscience. The publishing arm of the Maryknoll Fathers and Brothers, Orbis seeks to explore the global dimensions of the Christian faith and mission, to invite dialogue with diverse cultures and religious traditions, and to serve the cause of reconciliation and peace. The books published reflect the views of their authors and do not represent the official position of the Maryknoll Society. To learn more about Maryknoll and Orbis Books, please visit our website at www.maryknollsociety.org.

Copyright © 2010 by Gillian Crow.

Published by Orbis Books, Maryknoll, NY 10545-0302.

Manufactured in the United States of America.

Library of Congress Cataloging-in-Publication Data

Bloom, Anthony, 1914–2003.
    [Selections. 2010]
    Metropolitan Anthony of Sourozh : essential writings / selected with an introduction by Gillian Crow.
       p. cm. – (Modern spiritual masters series)
       ISBN 978-1-57075-866-9 (pbk.)
    1. Russkaia pravoslavnaia tserkov'–Doctrines. 2. Orthodox Eastern Church–Doctrines. I. Crow, Gillian. II. Title. III. Series.
BX597.B55A25 2010
230'.1947–dc22   2009041057

Contents

Sources

Metropolitan Anthony's Books

Beginning to Pray. New York: Paulist Press; first published in England as *School for Prayer.* London: Darton, Longman & Todd, 1970.

Courage to Pray, with Georges Lefebvre. London: Darton, Longman & Todd, 1973; Crestwood, N.Y.: St. Vladimir's Seminary Press, 1984.

Encounter. London: Darton, Longman & Todd, 2005.

God and Man. London: Darton, Longman & Todd, 1971.

The Living Body of Christ. London: Darton, Longman & Todd, 2008.

Living Prayer. London: Darton, Longman & Todd, 1966.

Meditations on a Theme. London: Mowbrays, 1971.

Our Life in God. London: Metropolitan Anthony of Sourozh Foundation, 2007, booklet.

Practical Prayer. Conciliar Press, 1989, booklet.

Anthology, Metropolitan Anthony a Contributor

Living Orthodoxy in the Modern /World, chapter on death and bereavement. London: SPCK, 1996.

Introductions to Other People's Books

The Way of a Pilgrim (Anon.). London: SPCK, Introduction to 1972 English edition.

Sermons

Sermons published online at the Metropolitan Anthony Foundation, *www.metropolit-anthony.orc.ru/eng.*

Unpublished Talks

Genesis, from a series of talks given at the Russian cathedral in London, 1990s.

Introduction

Metropolitan Anthony was one of the most respected church-men, spiritual writers, and broadcasters in Britain and Russia of the last few decades and one of the most prominent Ortho-dox personalities on the world stage. For over fifty years he was head of the Russian Orthodox Church in Great Britain under the Patriarchate of Moscow, where he was father to a multi-ethnic flock both at his cathedral in London and in parishes all over the country.

Born in Switzerland in 1914 into a Russian imperial diplo-matic family, he spent his early childhood in Persia until the 1917 Revolution made his father's imperial appointment there untenable. After an exciting journey to Europe his family set-tled in Paris, living in poverty among the large community of Russians who had fled the Revolution. On leaving school he trained to be a doctor and after World War II was ordained to the priesthood. Arriving in Britain in 1949 he played a major part in ecumenical work both there and abroad and had a great influence on many Anglican and other churchmen and women. As an Orthodox bishop he became a well-known speaker, broadcaster, and writer with a voice that was heard far beyond the bounds of his own Church. In Russia, which he vis-ited frequently, he developed a large following and was widely read, even in the days when it was dangerous to read his works.

For Metropolitan Anthony, Orthodoxy was not the reaction-ary force it is often taken to be, but the universal, undistorted message of the Gospel for all — a fact he brought alive in opening up his own diocese of the Russian Orthodox Church in Britain to people of every nationality and background. His books such as *Living Prayer, Beginning to Pray, God and Man* — later issued as the compendium *The Essence of*

Prayer — have become classics. For tens of thousands of readers the world over he spoke of prayer and the search for the living God whom he had come to know, in language that went to the heart of people, echoing their own longings. He was a spiritual guide not only to the many who knew him personally but also to all those by whom he was known through his writing and broadcasting.

He was also a great Orthodox thinker — a theologian not in the academic sense, which he was always quick to stress, but according to the beautiful definition of Evagrius of Pontus: "one who prays truly." His talks on the living out of the Christian life, with particular reference to Orthodoxy and its ecclesiology, were brought together in two books published posthumously in English: *Encounter* and *The Living Body of Christ*. He also contributed forewords to a number of books by other writers; preached numerous sermons, which are now being collected and distributed electronically; and gave frequent talks and lectures, some of which have already been printed in a variety of journals. There are also books published in Russian that are yet to be translated into English.

Except for the Russian books, the selections in this anthology are taken from all of the sources listed above, including some of his sermons. It is hoped that a collection of the latter will be published commercially before too long. The Metropolitan Anthony of Sourozh Foundation was set up to gather together his work and is in charge of promoting it and disseminating it to as wide an audience as possible.

Metropolitan Anthony was a warm, charismatic person, aglow with the joy of his faith, but also a man who endeavored to live out his vocation amid the turmoil of exile and busy parish life. His writings reflect both the essence of Orthodox Christianity and his own experience of the struggle to live that faith on a daily basis. His life as a child and as a young adult had been extremely hard, both physically and emotionally; and this harsh experience shaped his character and influenced his outlook. His writings are peppered with anecdotes from these early years and also from his work both as a priest and as a doctor, and they give an unforgettable immediacy to his words and make them highly readable, while at the same time conveying the depth of his inner life, his faith, and his commitment to God.

Metropolitan Anthony was born André Borisovich Bloom, the son of a Russian imperial diplomat and, on his mother's side, the nephew of the composer Alexander Scriabin. The Blooms were on leave in Lausanne, Switzerland, at his birth — June 19, 1914 — but were recalled to Moscow as war loomed. After some months André's father, Boris, was posted to Persia, where he continued his work in the diplomatic corps until the Bolsheviks seized power in Russia and, at the beginning of the 1920s, dismissed him.

During this time in Persia the young André enjoyed a happy and comfortable home life in grand embassy accommodations, surrounded by his loving parents and doting maternal grandmother. It was to be the only normal family home life he was to experience, and it ended abruptly when the Blooms were forced to leave Persia for exile and poverty.

Settling in Paris in 1923 after a sojourn in Vienna, and with the loss of their country, their status, and their financial and material assets, both Bloom parents struggled to make a living, taking on menial work to survive among the hundred thousand or so desperately poor Russian émigrés in the city at that time. From a sheltered privileged existence, the nine-year-old André found himself homeless, boarding in a slum school while his parents lodged wherever they could find a bed.

This had a profound effect on the young boy's emotional development. By temperament he was rather reserved. The horrors of merciless bullying at school turned him inward to become a loner, distrustful of everyone around him and seeing the world as a hostile place to be endured with a stony heart: it was the only way he could survive in his new, cruel circumstances. Never a believing child, he was further turned against religion and any idea of God by this harsh experience of life, and that antipathy was reinforced by what he saw of the Roman Catholicism and Protestantism around him.

André's focus in life became Russian patriotism, for which he found an outlet in the Russian Scout and youth movements spawned by the exiled community. He was sent away to their summer camps, which he was eventually to use as a model for the summer youth camp of his diocese in England.

The Russian Student Youth Movement and its camps included a certain amount of religious activity, towards which the young boy felt an immediate antipathy. However, when at the age of fifteen he finally became tempted — albeit with hostile intention — to read the Gospel, he unexpectedly but very soberly became aware of the presence of Christ in a manner so vivid that it left him in no doubt as to God's existence and God's love.

This experience, described in his own words in the first chapter of this book, changed his life irrevocably. From then on he dedicated himself to communing with Christ and, to the extent that he was able, to living according to his will. He began to pray, to read the Gospels, and to go to church. His natural inclination was to attend Russian Orthodox services, although he also investigated the other Churches and, as he later said, discovered in Orthodoxy what seemed to him to be the true and undistorted Christian faith.

André found a spiritual father, Father Afanasy (Nechaev) and set his heart on becoming a monk. Father Afanasy belonged to the only parish in Paris under the Moscow Patriarchate. The Alexander Nevsky Cathedral and the dozens of little Russian churches scattered across the city were in the jurisdiction of the Ecumenical Patriarchate, under whose *omophorion* (authority) they had come to seek refuge following Russia's Revolution and civil war. The small band of adherents to Moscow included a number of men who were to become renowned throughout Orthodoxy: among them Father Alexander Schmemann (later a founder of the Orthodox Church in America), the theologian Vladimir Lossky, and the icon painter Gregory Krug. This interwar period in Paris produced a great flowering of Orthodox thought and activity. Another of the young André's acquaintances was St. Maria of Paris (Mother Maria Skobtsova), whom he initially found totally uncongenial. An early recollection of her was of passing a sidewalk café where there was a table with a glass of beer on it, and behind it a Russian nun smoking a cigarette. This behavior shocked him. Later, however, he came to recognize her inner qualities, as she went around Paris helping the destitute and later aiding Jews to escape during the Nazi occupation of the city. She was finally sent to the Ravensbrück concentration camp, to die in the gas chambers.

Thwarted in his initial attempt to undertake training for the priesthood at the St. Sergius Theological Institute — André was told to go away, read the Greek Fathers, and come back in fifteen years' time — he decided on leaving school to put his Christian faith into practice by training as a doctor, with the intention of eventually becoming a worker priest in rural France. He studied physics, chemistry, and biology, and then medicine, at the Sorbonne, qualifying in 1939 just before the outbreak of the Second World War. Days before he was called up to serve in the medical corps of the French Army he asked Father Afanasy to receive his monastic vows. So began six years of medical work as a junior surgeon undertaken either in the army or, when France fell to the Germans, in hospitals in occupied Paris — all the while living an inner, secret life as a monk. He was to describe this apparent anomaly as excellent training for the monastic life, teaching him to accept the will of others and to put their needs before his own in the most practical way.

At the end of the war André entered general practice in Paris. He had come to realize that surgery was largely a matter of technique, while he felt called to a more personal relationship with his patients. During the war he had acquired a reputation for sitting with dying soldiers, and it was obvious that he had a gift for gentle, compassionate care. He kept a Bible in his surgery alongside his medical books.

His father had died, and he assumed the sole responsibility of living with and caring for his mother and grandmother. His spiritual father had also died, in 1943, shortly after he had tonsured André and given him the monastic name of Anthony. In 1948 he was at last ordained, expecting to continue his medical work in France. Instead, following a visit to England to the annual conference of the Anglican/Orthodox Fellowship of St. Alban and St. Sergius, Father Anthony was invited to return to England to work full-time for the Fellowship; and in January 1949 he and his family left France for good to settle in London. This was to be the end of his medical career. He did, however, continue throughout his life to consider himself to be a scientist and a doctor, and this had considerable influence on his thinking and on his pastoral work, particularly in the way that he always looked at the whole person, body and soul, and was quick to point out if he thought a person's spiritual malaise had a physical cause.

Father Anthony's work for the Fellowship allowed him to spend time serving in the Russian Patriarchal parish in London, where he became a popular figure. On the death of its parish priest in 1950 he became its full-time vicar, and he was to remain at its head until his own death more than fifty years later. Initially he spoke no English, but he set about learning the language. Bilingual in French and Russian from infancy, and speaking fluent German from early childhood, he soon made progress, and this enabled him to build up a rapport with the non-Orthodox English people he met through the Fellowship. He also became aware that the younger members of the Russian émigré families were being assimilated and marrying into the surrounding British culture and so were at home speaking English, and that this phenomenon would increase as time went on. There was a need among these young people for talks in English. Eventually some English also began to be used during the services, and by the end of Metropolitan Anthony's life every service at his cathedral in London contained an equal amount of Church Slavonic and English.

In December 1956 the parish moved into a rented Anglican church in Ennismore Gardens, Knightsbridge, and eventually bought the building in 1979. This was a courageous act — indeed, it was an act that seemed foolhardy to some of his congregation, who could not see how they could possibly take on such a responsibility. Father Anthony was convinced, however, that the presence of an outward-looking Orthodoxy, committed to bringing the faith to those beyond a select band of Russian émigrés, needed its own large physical base from which to set about its missionary task. And so what was to become the Russian cathedral in Knightsbridge, London, was purchased after an appeal that brought in funds not only from the parishioners, who made real sacrifices, but also from outside well-wishers, particularly the Anglicans.

Father Anthony had been consecrated bishop in 1957 and archbishop in 1962, on the creation of a new diocese to cover the territory of the British Isles. In 1966 he was raised to the rank of Metropolitan of Sourozh,* although he often referred to himself as, and many of his spiritual children still called him, "Father Anthony," to the end of his days. He remained the father of a growing family throughout his life, knowing his parishioners and members of his diocese by name, happy not only to give spiritual advice but also to receive criticism from them, and never putting on airs in private, however dignified he conducted himself during services. He also continued to live according to the principle he had agreed on with his mother in Paris at the end of the war: that as long as there remained one hungry person in the world, they would not live above the minimum level of food and shelter. He continued to live in that simple manner, which in his case had nothing to do with his monasticism and everything to do with his concern for the needs of others, for the rest of his life. He lived in a tiny flat at the back of the cathedral, acting as its unofficial caretaker, and he arranged diocesan finances so that he as a monk drew a smaller salary than his priests, who were married men with families to support.

As his command of English grew he became a popular broadcaster and was in demand as a speaker and preacher up and down the country. He gave guest lectures at universities all over Britain, often to medical students. People of all denominations warmed to him, and he to them. His aim was always to speak

---

*In the Russian Orthodox Church, a metropolitan is the rank above archbishop; Sourozh was the name given to Metropolitan Anthony's diocese; the name comes from a town in the Crimea.

from the heart to the hearts of his listeners, without any desire to convert but simply to bring the Gospel message to people and to bring those people to Christ. He spoke with fervor, with simplicity and sincerity, often with humor, and invariably without notes. The question sessions that usually followed always enlivened him, and he excelled at giving robust answers. Speaking off the cuff was a particular gift that he had nurtured ever since he had first given a talk in English and had been reprimanded by an Orthodox priest for his boring delivery. "From now on I order you to speak without notes," Father Lev Gillet had told him; and he became adept at speaking spontaneously, whether it was in giving sermons, lecturing, or broadcasting on radio or television.

His talks began to be recorded and transcribed and were eventually collected into a number of books on prayer. Because they were taken from the spoken word they retained an immediacy that not only made them easy to read, but also appealed to the hearts of his readers. He always directed what he said at himself as much as other people, using "we" instead of "you," and he often included anecdotes about his own life that gave them an intimate quality. Here were books that spoke not of theory but of practice, from a very personal angle, so that his readers could see that they were the product of real life and not just pious words thought up in a study. This proved immensely powerful. They were books that converted people. At first they appeared only in English, but they soon began to be translated into other languages and published — either legitimately, as for instance in France, or in Russia as samizdat (underground) publications, which were reproduced and passed from hand to hand in defiance of the Soviet authorities.

On his arrival in England, the young Father Anthony had found himself in a very different milieu from that of the Russian diaspora in Paris. Instead of the large numbers of Russian churches in France, he found only one small parish consisting largely of ageing émigrés in London, and an even smaller one in Oxford. During the next fifty years under his enthusiastic leadership, other communities sprang up in various parts of the country. Some of these consisted entirely of English people (including the priest) while others were mixed. His congregation at the cathedral in London included not only Russians and English converts, but Orthodox of many nationalities. The languages used for the services always reflected the local need. Most communities worshiped in borrowed buildings. There was a pioneering spirit, which was inspired by Metropolitan Anthony's vision of mission.

He was always quick to differentiate between mission and proselytism. The latter, according to his definition, was the attempt to convert people by forceful or underhand means such as the offering of material inducements. He had had some experience of this in prewar Paris, where the French Catholics tried to wean the Russians away from Orthodoxy by means such as offering places at their schools, provided the pupils converted. By contrast, he saw mission as the open proclamation of the Gospel, with no strings attached. So when in the latter years of his life a charity was set up by some of his flock to send material aid to Russia (the St. Gregory's Foundation), he was adamant that the aid should go to anyone in need, with no preconditions or inducements and with no discrimination between Orthodox and nonbelievers.

Over a period of forty years Metropolitan Anthony was a household name in Britain, broadcasting regularly on radio and television. His books sold in the thousands. Although the media sometimes tried to use him for political ends — the Cold War was at its height and any news of the Russian Church was always politicized — he kept himself resolutely beyond politics, which were never of great interest to him. His focus was always on Christ and the Gospel, and he abhorred any attempts at being used, by one side or the other.

He was able to visit Russia regularly, where he was shown around by officials so that he could see what the authorities wished him to see. However, he also conducted illegal meetings in private apartments, talked to clergy and worshipers behind the backs of his "minders," and spoke out in a forthright manner that Soviet citizens were not accustomed to hearing at all.

Small in stature, he was mighty in fearlessness and was prepared to stand up to anyone. The years of countering bullies at his school had borne useful fruit. He became a household name in Russia, too. His books and talks were passed around in samizdat copies, and thousands listened to his regular broadcasts on the BBC World Service or Radio Liberty. He once remarked with obvious glee that a niece in Russia had told him how these broadcasts were jammed by the Soviet authorities — but while the jamming worked in the old prerevolutionary apartment blocks, the flimsy construction of the modern Soviet buildings allowed the broadcasts to get through.

By the beginning of the 1990s the majority of the worshipers at his London cathedral were British converts to Orthodoxy, and it seemed that situation would continue. However, with the fall of the Soviet Union, large numbers of its citizens were able to travel to England, and many found their way, for religious or cultural reasons, to the Russian churches there, particularly in London. Metropolitan Anthony attempted to integrate them into the established community and convert them to his open, non-nationalistic understanding of Orthodoxy.

This period coincided with his advancing years and declining health. During this time Bishop Basil (Osborne), an American who had been one of his two assistant bishops, took over the day-to-day administration of the diocese.

In early 2003 Metropolitan Anthony announced his need to retire because he was suffering from cancer, for which he went on to have surgery and chemotherapy. His Diocesan Assembly met to approve his retirement and chose Bishop Basil as his successor. This choice was conveyed to Russia for approval by the Holy Synod of the Moscow Patriarchate.

That approval, given in late July just a matter of days before Metropolitan Anthony died, was only in the form of Bishop Basil's temporary appointment and not, as the Assembly had wished, as its permanent ruling bishop.

Metropolitan Anthony departed this life on August 4, 2003, at the age of eighty-nine and was buried with great ceremony, in the presence of a large number of the people who had revered him, on August 13. Bishop Basil was the chief celebrant, and addresses were given by the Anglican Archbishop of Canterbury, Rowan Williams; Archbishop Gregorios of the Greek Orthodox Archdiocese in Britain; and the Patriarchate of Moscow's representative, Metropolitan Filaret of Minsk. His grave, marked with a granite three-barred cross in the Russian manner, can be found in Brompton Cemetery, West London.

Metropolitan Anthony left a tangible legacy in his books, recorded talks, and sermons, more and more of which continue to be published. He also left the legacy of many thousands of people who had been touched by his words and who had become Christians, or had their faith strengthened, because of them — especially in Russia. His vision for an Orthodox community has been carried forward, first under Bishop Basil's leadership in the newly formed Vicariate of Parishes of Russian Tradition — formed from over half the old Diocese of Sourozh — as part of the Paris Exarchate of Russians under the protection of the Ecumenical Patriarch; and more recently, on Bishop Basil's retirement, as a Deanery within the Exarchate. The Diocese of Sourozh remains within the Moscow Patriarchate.

Metropolitan Anthony lived through a time — almost the whole of the twentieth century — when there was not only vast upheaval in the Russian Church, but also much turmoil and soul-searching in Christian churches everywhere. In Russia the church was first decimated by systematic state persecution following the 1917 Revolution and then, after the fall of the Soviet system in the early 1990s, reinvigorated. But it was also, to some extent, harnessed by the emerging political order for its own ends. Throughout, the Russian Church remained steadfast in its beliefs and doctrine, whatever faults it had. Other churches were faced with different problems, which were arguably more destructive than outright persecution: declining numbers, creeping apathy and secularism, and in some places an apologetic watering down of central beliefs and theology, which provoked public debate but failed to halt the decline in church

attendance. (The Orthodox Churches — which are a communion of national Churches sharing the same beliefs, services and
ecclesial structures — tend to be plagued not by arguments over
theology but by power struggles.)

Metropolitan Anthony remained true to Orthodox teaching,
which he was not afraid to proclaim in whatever situation he
found himself. As a teenager, having newly found Christ, he
would regale fellow travelers on the Paris Metro on his way
to school, asking them, "Have you discovered God? Have you
discovered the Gospels?" As a mature bishop in England several decades later he preached to longshoremen on the docks at
British ports. He challenged unbelievers in Soviet Russia and a
notable atheist of the day, Marghanita Laski, on English television. What he always aimed to do was not to preach Orthodoxy
as such, but to speak from the heart as a Christian from an
Orthodox perspective.

Orthodoxy is often thought by outsiders to be a backward-
looking faith, intent on sticking relentlessly to its tradition and
refusing to take any steps to become relevant to the modern
world. With its forms of worship apparently unchanged for
centuries, it is often compared to Roman Catholicism before
Vatican II — "Catholicism without the Pope" is a description
that has been used by some. This is a long way from reality.
True, the services do date from the early centuries of Christianity and the use of incense and chanting — albeit a very different
sound from Gregorian chant — gives the impression that this
Church is a long way from contemporary culture — the word
often used is "timeless," meant as a euphemism for being stuck
in a fourth-century time-warp.

In fact, the timelessness of Orthodoxy refers to the Kingdom
of God, a realm outside time, a realm where earthly considera-
tions — whether those of the fourth or twenty-first centuries —
do not hold sway. When we partake of one of our services we
are in the eternal "now," we share in an experience, however
veiled, of heaven on earth. At the Incarnation God became man;
he came down to us and to our level — in order to draw us up

to him; and our faith, our worship, our Christian life, are a participation in God's eternal life, in the wondrous "now" of the Kingdom, rather than in the world and its secular culture.

Thus the incense, the myriads of candles, the singing, the colorful icons and frescoes are not optional ornamentation. They are ways of using all our human senses to glorify God and to become aware that we are in his presence. Our worship exemplifies a sense of wholeness that runs through Orthodoxy. We do not like dividing worship from belief, body from soul, prayer from fasting, faith from works. Indeed, the word "Orthodoxy" is often described as meaning right faith and worship — not one or the other but both together. Our worship expresses our faith.

We experience how the lightness of fasting is an aid to prayer (conversely everyone knows the sluggishness produced by overeating). We understand how the body as well as the soul responds to God and will share in the Resurrection. We do not see the body as a temporary suit of clothes, defiled by sin, that becomes redundant at death. We remember that we are unique creatures of body and soul together, both destined for Eternity, and that Christ cared for the whole person, and healed bodies as well as souls. We are vividly aware that all our sins are committed with our bodies, but are moved by the desires of the soul; so they cannot be separated. Similarly, Orthodoxy has never been faced with the opposition of faith to works that caused such division in Western Christianity. We see faith and works as two sides of the same coin that cannot be separated.

These are just a few examples of the way in which the approach of the Orthodox differs from the Western Churches. In all of these matters, Metropolitan Anthony firmly upheld the Orthodox position; and as a doctor he was particularly close to the understanding of the human person as being a unique creature of body and soul together, both good, but in need of healing and salvation, and both inseparable in the spiritual life.

Metropolitan Anthony was able to keep himself outside power struggles because the Iron Curtain allowed him to order his diocese in Britain as he saw fit, free of Moscow's involvement. He was his own man and would brook no interference, although at the end of his life he was doubtless aware that in the new political circumstances in Russia, and with the ability of Russians to travel to the West in large numbers, that freedom would not continue after his death.

He had set up his diocese and had its statutes drawn up in close conformity to the Statutes of the Russian Church, which had been formulated in 1917–18 but never put into effect because of the Revolution and its aftermath. Perhaps the most controversial innovation, in the eyes of the Moscow Patriarchate, was the clause in his diocese's statutes giving it the right, through its Diocesan Assembly, to elect its own bishop. Such a practice was unknown in Russia, where the Holy Synod, under the watchful eyes of the State, made the choice.

Metropolitan Anthony spoke many times about this, and also about how he saw his diocese as an example for others to follow. He had an audacious vision of how a Christian body should be organized, and an audacious voice and spirit in promoting this vision. His understanding of the Church and its structures was a most important part of his legacy. It is a tragedy that it was so quickly buried by the very Patriarchate to whom he gave his allegiance. But it is vital that his vision is kept alive, and this book is an opportunity for people of the next generation to read of it and carry it forward.

It is sometimes said that while Catholics and Protestants have different answers to questions, the Orthodox have different questions. Metropolitan Anthony's own questions and answers about his faith, while always remaining true to Orthodoxy, were colored by the fact that he approached them not as a theologian but as a scientist. In modern parlance, he was not afraid to "think outside the box." Indeed, he was too big in heart and mind and faith for any box. He had a fearsome intellect, but he also laid great stress on personal experience, and the ability to be open to God's love and to bring it to other people. He shared the general Orthodox dislike and distrust of anything approaching casuistry. In many ways he felt closer to the Evangelicals than to Catholics or Anglicans.

He insisted that one must have a personal, living relationship with the Living God. Nothing less would do. This had to be centered on communing with him in prayer or silence. Since a relationship is always two-way, one had to learn to listen to God. In that respect, he encouraged people to shun the reading of pages and pages of prayers — something that Orthodox prayer books could easily encourage — and to make every word spoken, or every minute of silence, focused and meaningful. He was also anxious to discourage an excess of piety, to the extent of recommending his readers in *Beginning to Pray* to find a nickname for God and referring to the overzealous as having spiritual indigestion.

Although he had taken monastic vows, he never lived in a monastery, and so his spiritual life was akin to those of his listeners and parishioners — "in the market place," as he put it, surrounded by the same issues and problems that beset laypeople. Consequently his advice was never churchy or particularly "pious" — and he was fond of putting quote marks around that word. He would use anecdotes from his own life to illustrate how to live as a Christian in the modern world. An example: he once described how as a student he was irritated by his grandmother's repeated insistence on closing his bedroom window while he was out. He overcame his irritation not through prayer but by betting with himself that she would close the window, and so winning the psychological battle.

If the Orthodox have different questions from Catholics and Protestants, they sometimes have no questions at all. This is largely the case with reference to the ordination of women, which has not arisen spontaneously within Orthodoxy but has been posed from the outside. With the ordination of women by the Anglicans, this question began to be put to the Orthodox, and in most places received an answer that was, as Metropolitan Anthony said, a gut reaction made with very little thought behind it. He, on the contrary, did think, and was one of the first notable Orthodox clergymen to suggest that there was, as far as he could see, no reason why women could not be ordained. This led to his being demonized in some quarters, while other people tried to soften his words by saying he did not really mean what he said. But he repeated his championing of women's causes on many occasions, characteristically not being at all afraid to stick his neck out. He once claimed, jokingly, that he would be burned as a heretic on a pyre made from the complete works of Metropolitan Anthony. Notably, he gave vocal support to the writings of the French Orthodox theologian Elisabeth Behr-Sigel. He also advanced the position of women in his own diocese. At one time both the chair of the Diocesan Assembly and the diocesan secretary, two key administrative posts, were held by women. He encouraged women to write and speak publicly on the Orthodox Church and Orthodox issues. The chief layperson at his cathedral was for many years a woman. As a corollary to this, he was anxious for men to share the menial tasks in the church. For instance, at his annual diocesan conference he might give a deacon the job of clearing the tables after meals, citing the first deacons in the Book of Acts. He was also not above doing such things himself, offering to wash the dishes while mothers listened to a talk for parents and daily performing the duties of caretaker at his own cathedral. Until late middle age he would spend Easter Day scraping candle wax off the cathedral floor. He valued both men and women, but expected them to have equal humility.

Metropolitan Anthony was renowned as a spiritual father. His fame as a confessor spread far beyond his own diocese, and there was a continual host of people clamoring to see him. He was a charismatic figure, larger than life in every respect but physical size. Even nonbelievers who met him were struck by something in him that they recognized as being out of the ordinary, even if they were not able to define it as the Holy Spirit. He was not something who could be easily ignored or forgotten. There were also times when he made mistakes, practical and spiritual, and he could on occasion upset people badly. Being larger than life affected all aspects of his personality.

He held the firm belief that encounter with God had to be an exercise of total commitment demanding 100 percent dedication to God. A half-hearted, lukewarm Christianity was, in his mind, worse than useless. He once said on a radio program, when the interviewer suggested his uncompromising stance might frighten people off, that it would be a blessing if some people were frightened off and if those who stayed were to take their faith much more seriously. This was during the 1980s, at a time when the churches around him were bending over backward in a desperate attempt to accommodate themselves to secular society in order to halt the decline in Church attendance. That decline continued, while Metropolitan Anthony's own congregation increased steadily, roused by his call for people to accommodate themselves to God.

In his spiritual counsel he did not necessarily set out to give people answers, but to provoke questions. He saw no profit in telling people what to believe; he preferred them to work things out for themselves. He was aware that it was far more important for them to have an experience of God's love than to hear a priest give endless sermons on it. Many people, on meeting him, felt the love of God through him. And he expected his spiritual children, and the readers of his books, to respond in turn to God's love by becoming its vehicles themselves. Each day one was to go out into the world to be the presence of the Gospel, the presence of Christ, as he said in *Beginning to Pray*.

But before that one had to find God. Metropolitan Anthony talked almost as much about God's absence as he did about his presence; and he saw this absence not as something to be brushed under the carpet, a source of embarrassment, but as a starting point for finding God. No one ever had to pretend to him that they had more faith than they had. To the complete unbeliever in Russia who told him arrogantly, "I don't believe in God," he could reply, "Well, that's your loss!" But to anyone who came to him genuinely lamenting their lack of faith he would take their side and gently lead them to see that this absence was something real and to be valued. In the opening chapter of *Beginning to Pray* he went into detail about the positive side of the absence of God. And this was exactly where many people, under his guidance, began their journey towards a living faith.

The core of his work remains the books on prayer, and inevitably selections from these little books make up a large part of this volume. Metropolitan Anthony had a habit of repeating himself. This had nothing to do with his advancing years but had always been a feature of his talks and writings. He told the same anecdotes about his own life over and over, and in each book they reappear, perhaps in a slightly different form, leaving no one to say for certain which account of any particular incident corresponded most closely to what had actually happened. In any case, that is irrelevant. What matters is always the kernel of truth at the heart of the story, told to get across a point that might otherwise have been ignored. In other words, he used anecdotes as parables. In the tradition of the Gospel parables, they reach out to people in a way that serious prose can never do.

I have included in this volume a number of his sermons. They used to be published in his monthly *Cathedral Newsletter* during his life and are now available from the Metropolitan Anthony Foundation website (where one can subscribe to a weekly sermon email). These are generally, but not always, short — Metropolitan Anthony said many times that no sermon should last more than ten minutes, because after that, people simply switched off. Indeed, contrary to what often appears to be thought in the Russian Church, where sermons can go on and on, great skill is needed to get across a message in just a few words. Metropolitan Anthony was indeed skilful in presenting powerful sermons that exhorted his hearers to take the Gospel to heart. Usually they were encouraging pieces. His parishioners would leave the cathedral feeling uplifted by his words. Sometimes, however, they demanded a challenging response, perhaps repentance — and this always included himself. True to Orthodox tradition the sermons were generally based on the day's Gospel reading, although occasionally there would be some pressing issue on Metropolitan Anthony's mind about which he would speak. He always spoke, as he did at other times, without any notes. He might claim afterwards that a particular sermon was the product of absolutely no forethought, although on other occasions it was clear that he had spent time thinking about the passage beforehand. Because the Sunday Gospel readings occur again and again in successive years, he was mainly limited to a certain number of themes on which to preach, leaving him with not much that was new to say at the end of his ministry. Often what he did say was so passionately delivered that it had a tremendous impact at the time, but looked less outstanding in print. Yet if these sermons are read with the same open heart with which they were spoken, they will hit home in the way in which they were intended.

Metropolitan Anthony was a poor correspondent and kept no diary beyond an appointments book, so there are no letters or journal entries here, and no plans for anything of that nature to be published. His handwriting was beautiful but executed very slowly, and he was a two-finger typist on a very old machine, so he found putting things down on paper a chore. That is also one of the reasons why he wrote no books himself. He left it to others to gather up his words and get them into print; and in his later years he was more inclined to favor publication of his Russian-language talks, because it was in Russia that he felt that the need for his message was greatest.

I have edited the selections as little as possible. Metropolitan Anthony's English, delivered in a sonorous Franco-Russian accent, was excellent to a point. He had a very good command of English idioms and slang; but he also had his own idioms that he never ironed out, fearing that if he perfected his English too much he might be in danger of losing his Russian, which he spoke elegantly and about which he was passionate. So his version of the English language came to be known among his parishioners as "Anthonian English." Some of its idiosyncrasies were corrected by his transcribers, but I have not attempted to remove any more. In any case, one of the sources, the posthumous book *Encounter,* is translated (by the Pushkin authority Tatiana Wolff) from the original Russian.

Metropolitan Anthony was a great admirer of Father Alexander Schmemann, the Orthodox writer and founding father of the OCA (Orthodox Church in America), and he urged his congregation to read Schmemann's books. They had both learned their faith in prewar Paris, and both were passionate about the Orthodox Church's vocation to spread its message to all people regardless of nationality. With the understanding that many of the Russian exiles living in Paris at that time had, they saw the Russian emigration as a God-given opportunity to bring the treasure of Orthodoxy to the non-Orthodox world. They had, they said, been scattered like seeds over the earth in order to grow and bring forth fruit. So they both spoke with the voice of a universal Christianity, with a message and a style that was readily accessible to everyone. I hope that people reading this book and meeting Metropolitan Anthony for the first time will hear something of that message and take it to heart.

1

Faith in the Gospel

The central event of Christianity, and the focus of the Gospels, is the Resurrection of the Lord Jesus Christ. The Orthodox Church sings of the Resurrection not only on Easter night — repeating over and over again the Easter hymn, "Christ is risen from the dead, trampling down death by death, and to those in the tombs he has given life" — but every Sunday. It never forgets that this is the central event of the Christian faith, indeed, without which there would be no Church and no Christian faith. Nor is the Resurrection watered down to mean only some kind of spiritual resurrection. It is the bodily Resurrection of which the Orthodox Church sings, of which Orthodox preachers preach and writers write.

Metropolitan Anthony was no exception. It is fitting, then, to begin this book with his own certainty in the Resurrection, and his own experience of it.

Some people, while admiring the importance of the Resurrection in the experience of the Apostles, wonder how this apostolic experience can have the same central significance for us; but is it enough for us simply to believe in the words of others and to found our faith on something totally unverifiable? I would like to stress the fact that, of all the historic events in the world, the Resurrection of the Lord belongs equally to past history and to present reality. Christ, dead on the cross on one particular day, Christ, risen from the tomb in his glorified, human flesh on one particular day, belongs to the past as a historic fact; but Christ, once risen, living forever in the glory of the Father, belongs to the history of each day and each instant, because being alive, according to his promise, he is with us, now and always. Christian experience from this point of view is essentially attached to the event of the Resurrection, because it is the one event in the Gospels that can become part of our own personal experience. All the rest we receive from tradition, written or spoken — the account of the Crucifixion, the different events told us by Holy Scripture — but the Resurrection, this we know personally, or else we are ignorant of the primordial, essential fact of the Church's life and the Christian faith. St. Symeon the New Theologian said: "How can one who knows nothing of the Resurrection in this life, expect to discover and enjoy it in his death?" Only the experience of the Resurrection and eternal life can make the death of the body into sleep and death itself into the Gate of Life.

If such a plain, peremptory statement arouses questions, demands a response, demands of you that you ask yourselves whether you are within Christian experience, so much the better! Here is the central experience without which there are no Christians, there is no Christianity, without which our faith is not faith but credulity; not "the certainty of things unseen" but the capacity to accept the witness of others, an unverifiable witness, a witness based on nothing more than that someone has said something that seems incredible but that, nevertheless, for reasons equally incredible, we are prepared to accept.

— *Meditations on a Theme*, 111

FINDING FAITH

Metropolitan Anthony's own faith in the Resurrection sprang from his first encounter with the Gospel as a teenager. While reading St. Mark — not out of piety, but rather in a spirit of radical skepticism — he became strikingly aware of Christ's presence. This was the great turning point in his life. Although he kept the actual experience to himself for years, he eventually recounted it during an ecumenical meeting, when he was already a priest in England, and subsequently he retold it many times, to individuals, in broadcasts, in talks, and in his books.

Before his conversion, however, he was hostile to any form of religion. This sprang largely from his difficult childhood, during which he was unhappy and endured a level of poverty that is unknown in the West today. His only experiences of religion were entirely negative.

As far as the Church was concerned, I was very against it, because of what I had seen among my friends, both Catholic and Protestant. God did not exist for me, and the Church was simply a negative phenomenon.

... I must say that I was not the only one who felt like that; in the summer in camp, there was Vespers on Saturdays, and a Liturgy on Sundays, and we *systematically* did not get up to go to the Liturgy and turned back the flaps of our tent so that those in charge could see that we were lying in bed and *not going anywhere*. So the foundation for religion in my life was an extremely doubtful one.

... In 1927 there was a priest at the children's camp who seemed to us very aged. He was probably about thirty years old, but he had a large beard and long hair, sharp features, and one characteristic that none of us could explain: and that was that he loved everybody. He did not love us in response to love or affection being shown to him; he did not love us as a reward for being "good" or obedient or anything of that kind. It was simply that his heart overflowed with love. Everybody could share in it, and not just a fraction or a drop, and it was never withdrawn. The one thing that did happen was that this love for a certain boy or girl was for him either a source of joy or of great sorrow. These were two aspects of the same love; it never lessened, and it never wavered. Indeed if one were to read what the Apostle Paul wrote of love: "Charity ... believeth all things, hopeth all things ... never faileth," all this could be found in him, although I did not understand this at that time. I knew that my mother loved me, that my father loved me, that my grandmother loved me, but that was the extent of the circle in my life as far as tender feelings went. But why a person who was a stranger to me could love me and could love others who were also strangers to him, was an idea that was foreign to me. It was only many years later that I understood where all this sprang from. But at the time it was a question mark in my consciousness, a question that could not be answered.

—*Encounter*, 191

Up to the age of fifteen life had been very hard; we had no common roof and I was at boarding school that was rough and violent. All the members of my family lived in different corners of Paris. It was only when I was about fourteen that we all gathered under a common roof, and that was real happiness and bliss. It is odd to think that in a suburban house in Paris one could discover perfect happiness but it was so. This was the first time that we had had a home since the Revolution. . . . When I found myself confronted with perfect happiness, a quite unexpected thing happened. I suddenly discovered that if happiness is aimless, it's unbearable. I could not accept aimless happiness. Hardships and suffering had to be overcome; there was always something beyond them. But because it had no further meaning and because I believed in nothing, happiness seemed to be stale. So I decided I would give myself a year to see whether life had any meaning. If in the course of that year I could not find any meaning, I decided I would not live; I would commit suicide.

. . . I began to look for a meaning in life other than what I could find through purposefulness. Studying and making oneself useful for life didn't convince me at all. All my life up to now had been concentrated on immediate goals, and suddenly these became empty. I felt something immensely dramatic inside myself, and everything around me seemed small and meaningless.

Months passed and no meaning appeared on the horizon. One day — it was during Lent, and I was then a member of one of the Russian youth organizations in Paris — one of the leaders came up to me and said, "We have invited a priest to talk to you, come." I answered with violent indignation that I would not. I had no use for the Church. I did not believe in God. I did not want to waste any of my time. The leader was subtle. He explained that everyone who belonged to my group had reacted in exactly the same way, and if no one came we would all be put to shame because the priest had come and we would be disgraced if no one attended his talk. "Don't listen," the leader said, "I don't care, but just sit and be a physical presence." That much loyalty I was prepared to give to my youth organization, so I sat through the talk. I didn't intend to listen. But my ears pricked up. I became more and more indignant. I saw a vision of Christ and Christianity that was profoundly repulsive to me. When the lecture was over I hurried home in order to check the truth of what he had been saying.   — *Beginning to Pray,* x

I asked my mother for a New Testament, which she did have, and I tucked myself away in my corner, looked at the book, and found that there were four Gospels, and as there were four of them one of the four must be shorter than the others. As I did not expect any good to come from any of the four, I decided to read the shortest one. And there I fell into a trap — as I was to discover many times in the future how cunning God is when he casts his nets in order to catch a fish — because had I read a different Gospel I would have had difficulties. Each Gospel has a certain cultural foundation: Mark, however, wrote exactly for young savages like me — for Roman youngsters. I did not know this, but God knew it, and maybe Mark knew it when he wrote more briefly than the others.

So I sat down to read. And at this point you will have to trust my word because this cannot be proved. Something happened to me that occasionally happens in the street, when you are walking along and suddenly you turn around because you think that someone behind you is looking at you. I was sitting and reading, and between the beginning of the first and the beginning of the third chapter of the Gospel according to St. Mark, which I was reading slowly because the language was unfamiliar to me, I suddenly felt that there, at the other side of the table, stood Christ. This feeling was so intense that I had to stop reading and look. I looked for a long time and I did not see anything, did not hear anything, nor did I feel anything. But even when I looked straight ahead of me at the place where there was nobody to be seen, I still had the same vivid sense that Christ was without any doubt standing there. I remember that at that point I leaned back and thought: if the living Christ is standing here — it means that he is the risen Christ. It means that I know personally and for certain, within the limits of my own, personal experience, that Christ has risen and that means that everything that is said about him is true.

— Encounter, 197

It was in the light of the Resurrection that I could read with certainty the story of the Gospel, knowing that everything was true in it because the impossible event of the Resurrection was to me more certain than any event of history.... I became absolutely certain within myself that Christ is alive and that certain things existed. I didn't have all the answers, but having touched that experience, I was certain that ahead of me there were answers, visions, possibilities. This is what I mean by faith — not doubting in the sense of being in confusion and perplexity, but doubting in order to discover the reality of life, the kind of doubt that makes you want to question and discover more, that makes you want to explore.   *— Beginning to Pray,* xii

What also astonished me at the time, and which I would probably have expressed quite differently then, is that God — and this is the very nature of love — is able to love us so much, that he is prepared to share everything with us to the last: not only creation through his Incarnation, not only the limiting of life through sin, not only physical suffering and death, but that which is the most terrible — mortality as a state of being, hell as a state of being: the deprivation and loss of God, from which man dies. That cry of Christ's on the cross: "My God! My God! Why hast Thou forsaken me?" — this experience not only of being abandoned by God but also of being deprived of God, which kills a man, this readiness of God to share our loss of God, as if descending with us into hell, because Christ's descent into hell was precisely a descent into the Old Testament abyss, that is, to the place where God is not. This amazed me because it meant that there was no limit to God's readiness to share man's fate, in order to find man. When very soon after this I entered the Church, I found that my personal experience was the experience of a whole generation of people, who before the Revolution had known the God of great cathedrals and of solemn services, who had then lost everything — their motherland, their loved ones, and often their self-esteem, their sense of their place in life, that gave them the right to life — who were deeply wounded and therefore so vulnerable. They suddenly discovered that through his love for man God wanted to become just as they were: defenseless, totally vulnerable, weak, powerless, and despised by those people who believe only in the triumph of might. I then became aware of an aspect of life that means a great deal to me: that our God, the Christian God, can not only be loved, but can be respected: that one can bow down to him, not only because he is God, but out of a feeling — and I can find no other words for it — of deep respect.

— Encounter, 199

DOUBT

Despite his own certainty, or perhaps because of it, Metropolitan Anthony was very much aware that for many people, doubt remained a huge obstacle in their spiritual lives. He never tried to push this issue, and the relationship between doubt and faith, under the carpet, or dress doubt up in pious words, as some preachers do. His approach was honest, direct, and bold, and it proved a great help to those who heard his words.

CREATIVE DOUBT

I would like to focus attention on perplexity and on doubt, in an attempt to provoke thought about a few words like faith, doubt, reality, and truth. I am not a theologian; I am a scientist by training, and a physician, so you will not find in my words any depth of philosophical probing into things. I am writing as an ordinary human being who is confronted with life and its problems.

First of all, concerning faith, one preliminary remark. Faith is very often understood by people as a defeat of intelligence. In other words, faith begins when I can no longer think creatively, when I let go of any attempt at rational understanding, and when I say "I believe" because it is so absurd that it is the only way of facing the problem. This may be an act of credulity, it may be an act of cowardice, it may be a preliminary act, full of wisdom and intelligence, that teaches us not to draw conclusions or to come to conclusions before we have understood. But this is not faith as understood by the great men of all religions, and particularly the Christian faith. In the Epistle to the Hebrews in the eleventh chapter, faith is defined as "certainty of things unseen." We usually lay the stress on "things unseen" and forget the "certainty" about them. So when we think of faith we usually think of the invisible and instead of certainty put against it a question mark. Then to solve the problem, we accept in a childish way, in an unintelligent way, very often what we are told by others — usually our grandparents of three generations back, or whoever else we choose to believe for reasons that are not always reasonable. But if you try to see the way in which faith originates in those people who were the great men of faith, the heroes of faith, you can see that it always originates in an experience that makes the invisible certain, and allows them, having discovered that the invisible is as real as the visible, to go further in searching the invisible by methods of their own.

There is a passage, for instance, in the works of Macarius of Egypt, a man who lived in the fourth century. He says, "The experience of God, the vision of the world in God, is something that can happen only at a moment when all our thoughts, all emotions, are arrested to such a degree that we can no longer both be within the experience, perceive the things, and step out of the experience, watch ourselves and analyze what is going on. The moment when an experience is 'lived' is a moment when we cannot observe it." And he says that this would be quite sufficient for someone who has had an experience of God. He would not wish to go back to another stage. But he also says, "God has concern, not only for those who have this experience, but also for the people who haven't got it; that someone should come to them as a witness of things unseen, and yet experienced and real, and he steps back away from them." At that moment begins, as he says, the realm of faith. The certitude remains even though the experience is already of the past; the certainty is there because what has happened to him is as certain as anything around him, is tangible, visible, perceived by the senses, so that the moment of faith begins as a result of a first contact with the invisible, discovered, disclosed somehow.

That means that we must be very severe and sober when we speak of our faith, for we often say "I believe this and that" when we have taken it from someone else that it is true. We don't care to investigate it in depth, and as long as this truth, or illusory truth is not destroyed or broken down, then we take it for granted. This is a bad faith; this is what one of our Russian theologians called "the aged sacrament of the faith that does not think."

What we *should* do whenever we are faced with that kind of faith is to confront it with experience. We ask ourselves whether we have any experience of it. If we haven't, it must remain a field to be investigated. It remains a field that was conveyed to us by someone who knows, but that is not known to us. It is promising, but it must hold its promise in the future. We cannot yet say, "I know, I am certain, I understand with experience."

This kind of faith — the faith of one who simply takes things on trust — sooner or later will be badly battered by life and by problems, by doubt in fact, or if you prefer, by perplexity. What happens so often with people is that when they are young, they are given a number of certainties that they accept on trust from their parents, their teachers, their surrounding, the milieu in which they live. After that, this minimum of faith is kept as a sort of treasure. We develop in all sorts of ways, but our awareness of the world invisible and of the certainties it entails does not grow with it. A moment comes around the age of eighteen, perhaps earlier or later, when a child in us, the little child of eight who has collected all the faith he was capable of and formed a world outlook which is childish, is confronted with an opponent, an adversary within himself. A girl, a young man, of eighteen, twenty, or twenty-five, says, "Nonsense, you can't believe that," and then an argument starts that is doomed to lead to the defeat of faith simply because it is the argument between a little child with a pure heart and uninvolved thinking and someone who poses to the childish nature the problems of another age, another level of understanding, another level of perception of the world.

At eight the world can be taken on trust; at eighteen, at twenty-five, it cannot; and in certain circumstances, there are things that can never be taken on trust. I will give you an example. The Eucharist, the central event of Christian worship, is centered on an act of thanksgiving in which we say to God "Thank you for all things." Now, can we honestly say, "Thank you for all things" in the face of the tragedies of the world unless we have a reason to see beyond the tragedy to their solution and a meaning within them?

Doubt is not simply contradiction. Doubt is a moment of dividedness, a dichotomy in our minds; a moment when, having followed a very simple straight road, we come to a fork, and we ask ourselves "Do I go this way or that way?" The one may be more convincing, the other may be more alluring. Which one are we going to choose? It is the situation of someone who has been weighing up the problems of life in a very simple way and suddenly discovers there is a much more subtle balance between things and that a simple solution is no solution at all. What are we going to do at that moment?

There are two absolutely different attitudes to doubt in the mind: there is that of the scientist and that of the believer. For the scientist, doubt is a systematic weapon; it is a joy. For the believer when he takes the wrong attitude to doubt and to the problems he is facing, it is a moment of anguish. What happens usually to the believer is that having believed in all simplicity that everything is clear, simple, straightforward, he suddenly discovers that life gives the lie to what he thought to be true. Then his answer is, "I am disloyal to what I thought, I am disloyal to my faith, to my Church, to my God." The problem is not only about subtleties but about basic things, about God himself, about the Church, about what is at the core of the believer's life. Then he feels that what is at stake is the breaking down, the destruction, the disappearance of the object of faith, and God's existence is now questionable. The values that were essential, that were existential values for him are questionable, and therefore his very existence becomes a problem and seems to be insuperably problematic.

But when a scientist engages in research, he gathers together all the facts he is capable of collecting. Once he has gathered his facts, he must hold them together in a way that makes it possible for him to handle the totality of the facts, and he builds a hypothesis, a theory, a model, a construction, an architectural building, that is capable of holding everything together. If the whole object of research for the scientist was to make himself a name, he will try to protect his model against any criticism, against any doubt, and against any questioning, with greater or lesser honesty. But if as a scientist he is a man who is out to discover what things are in reality, his first action will be to go around and around his model in all directions, examining and trying to find where the flaw is, what the problems are that are generated by the model he has built, by the theory he has proposed, by the hypothesis he has now offered for the consideration of others. If he cannot find a flaw, then he will try through research to go farther in the field and discover such facts that do not fit with his theory or his model, because when he will find a fact that will explode his model, make his theory questionable, he will have opened up a new window on reality. So the aim of the good research scientist is to create models of theories or hypotheses as a preliminary exercise to questioning and to discovering something that will make him break them down in order to create another model that is as doubtful as the preceding one, but that allows him to keep the new facts together in a manageable way.

At the root of the scientist's activity there is the certainty that what he is doubting is the model he has invented — that is, the way in which he has projected his intellectual structures on the world around him and on the facts, the way in which his intelligence has grouped things. But what he is also absolutely certain of is that the reality beyond his model is in no danger if his model collapses. The reality is stable, it is there; the model is an inadequate expression of it, but the reality doesn't alter because the model shakes.

"Model" can be replaced by another word when it is not used in a scientific way; it can be replaced by the word "truth." Truth is something that is an expression of reality, and an expression means two things: first, that the reality that surrounds us is perceived (obviously incompletely); second, that it is expressed (also incompletely, because of our inability to express identically in words and in expressions). Only one occasion in human history sees the moment when truth and reality coincide. That moment is in the incarnate Christ, because he is God, the plenitude, the fullness of creation, and at the same time the perfect expression of it. Then truth no longer answers the question "What?" It answers the question "Who?" and when Pilate said, "What is truth?" Christ gave him no answer for the simple reason that if he had said to him what he had said to the disciples, "I am the Truth," Pilate would have understood even less than the disciples, and the disciples understood nothing at that particular moment.

Truth and the expression of it is bound to be formulated in human terms, in the language of a given tribe, a nation, an epoch, and so forth. Obviously, it is limited but it has also another quality: truth can be either static or dynamic. You can express the truth in two ways. A snapshot is true and yet it is perfectly untrue. Everyone must have seen snapshots of preachers, lecturers, or politicians delivering a speech. They are usually taken at a moment when the subjects stand with their mouths open like a hippopotamus. Well, the snapshot is perfectly true, but it expresses only a split second and gives you a ridiculous image of something that perhaps at that moment was profoundly moving for the people. It is a petrification, a sort of fossil of something dynamic; it is true, and yet it does not express the truth because the truth at that moment was emotion. When you want to express the truth — that is, reality — dynamically, you discover that the truth becomes a problem of a quite different sort. Perhaps an example or two will explain what I mean.

There is a painting by the French painter Géricault called *The Derby at Epsom*. If you look at the painting, you will see that the horses are galloping, but if you are interested in zoology or in the mechanics of movement and examine the horses, you will discover that no horse gallops that way. Some are spread out in such a way that if they went on they would fall flat on their bellies; others stand with their four feet gathered together and couldn't even jump from the position in which they are painted. But what was Géricault aiming at? He aimed at showing the gallop and not the anatomy, the physiology. And he chose deliberately (because he knew perfectly well how to draw a horse) to falsify things as the only way of convincing the viewer that the horses were moving.

This is what we are always doing in theology or philosophy: we falsify things when we want to convey a dynamic moment, but often the reader takes them to be an adequate and immobile picture of what reality is. This is true for instance, of the Trinity.

...Reality is something within us that is the total thing that includes God and all things visible and invisible. This is what we aim at expressing in glimpses when we speak in terms of truth. These terms of truth may be inadequate; they are never identical with their object. In the field of art something very interesting may be discovered in the works of primitive painters, particularly of one Russian painter called Rublev, who lived six hundred years ago. He was trained by a man who had mastery of three-dimensional painting, and strangely enough, for most of his painting he reverted to two-dimensional. A Soviet historian of art made a study of the problem, and he showed that Rublev expresses all historical events in three dimensions, because particularly in time and in space they have thickness. But things that belong to the eternal he expresses only in two dimensions because they have no thickness; they are not within time and within space. When you look out of the window during the night in a thunderstorm, you may see the scenery in a flash — but it goes so quickly that you can't see whether one tree is farther or nearer than another, or any so precise detail. This is the way the truth is inadequate, that our intellectual, philosophical, theological, scientific model is inadequate in comparison with reality; it simply means that we are saying, "How marvelous, I have come to a point when I can outgrow the limitations in which I have lived and I can move into a greater, deeper, more enthralling vision of things as they are."

If we think of a scientist and a believer, then we will see that the scientist's doubt is systematic, it is surging, it is hopeful, it is joyful, it is destructive of what he has done himself because he believes in the reality that is beyond and not in the model he has constructed. This we must learn as believers for our spiritual life both in the highest forms of theology and in the small simple concrete experience of being Christian. Whenever we are confronted with a crossroads, whenever we are in doubt, whenever our mind sees two alternatives, instead of saying, "Oh God, make me blind, Oh God help me not to see, Oh God give me loyalty to what I know now to be untrue," we should say, "God is casting a ray of light which is a ray of reality on something

I have outgrown — the smallness of my original vision. I have come to a point when I can see more and deeper, thanks be to God." That is not perplexity, it is not bewilderment, it is not the anguished doubt of the believer who hides his head and hopes that he will be able to revert to the age of eight.

This is very important because unless you are prepared to see reality and your own thoughts and the thoughts of others with keen interest, with courage, but with the certainty that the last word is not doubt, not perplexity and not bewilderment, but that it is discovery, then you are wasting your time. You will die in the way in which in ancient mythology we are told: an ass that stood between a bucket of water and some straw and could never decide whether he was more hungry than thirsty or more thirsty than hungry. — *God and Man*, 32

I believe that in our day we still live under the illusion that everything that is not rational is dubious. And yet psychology has shown us that there is a whole irrational world that is decisive in a man's inner life. When I say "irrational" I do not mean "unreasonable." There is, for instance, the entire range of human love, whether it be friendship, family love, the love that singles out from the crowd the one who is unique for us, who reorientates the whole world for us. As one of the old Greek writers has said: "Before a man meets and loves the girl who will be his betrothed, he is surrounded by men and women; from the moment he discovers the beloved — it is *she* and the others are people." This experience, so rich, so complex, and so universal, belongs to the order of the irrational in the sense that it cannot be manufactured by reason: to love someone is not a balance sheet of reasons for and against; it is a direct experience, a fact that imposes itself but that goes too deep for us to be able to speak of any reasoned argument. It is the same with the experience of beauty, whether it is in music or the plastic arts, whether it depends on the ear or the eye; it is not just the sum total of good reasons for admiring a work of art. If we wish to share with someone our experience of the beauty of a piece of music, of sculpture, of architecture, or of painting we begin by inviting them with the words Christ spoke to his first disciples: "Come and see!" We certainly would not begin by saying: "First I am going to explain to you all the beauty in this work of art, and when you understand it properly, then you can be allowed to experience it."   — *Meditations on a Theme*, 31

HUMILITY AND READING THE GOSPELS

Very often people read the Gospels and mark in them the passages that strike them, as if revealing their own sinfulness or untruthfulness. I think that that serves no useful purpose: it only drives people to despair. When one looks at oneself and thinks: "I am not all that nice to know," that is already rather bad; but when one looks in the mirror of the Gospels, and it seems that God himself is saying to you: "Look how spiritually ugly you are!" — then there is indeed nothing to support you. So my advice is: read the Gospels and mark everything to which you feel affinity. When we read a certain section, we can have three kinds of reaction. There are places which hardly affect us: of course Christ knows best, and therefore he is probably right, but this does not touch me. Mentally it might be acceptable, but it does not disturb me. There are places — if we are absolutely honest — about which we would say: "Oh no, Lord! Oh no, this is not for me!"

I remember one old lady who came to a series of talks I gave on the Beatitudes. When we reached "Blessed are you when you are persecuted," she said to me, "Well, Father Anthony, if you call this being blessed, I will leave you to it. I have suffered enough. I do not want to hunger, or to feel cold, or to be persecuted — enough of that!" She was being honest, but we are not always so honest. We very often behave in exactly this way, but we do not say it to God, and we do not say it to ourselves: we only try to edge past such places. So one has to be honest, and, on the other hand, search for the places that speak of the beauty already in us, of things that already exist between God and us. While we are in agreement only to the extent of "If God says so, it must be true" — it has not yet reached us. But if we can say to God: "How splendid that is!" — it means we have met God in this saying, in this image, in this sermon, in this commandment. We can be overcome with joy, delight, and, like the travelers at Emmaus, exclaim: "Did not our heart burn within us, while he talked to us on the road?" (Luke 24:32). In our terms, this will mean that when we read a selection and can say, "Lord, how splendid this is! My God, how wonderful this is!" we have understood something. And if this happens even for a moment we can say: "I have discovered my kinship with God." If one thinks of oneself as a very spoiled and damaged icon, it means: "Here there is a remnant within me, an undamaged remnant of God's image, and I must cherish it as a holy commandment, for in this I am already in harmony with God. If I break this, I not only break my relationship with God, but I also destroy that which is already godly and holy within me." And this is the beginning of asceticism, because these little, let us say, stars in the sky must be defended from being destroyed in any way. They are like embers in the hearth that we can put out; and asceticism consists in defending these embers, as it were to feed them, so that the flame will grow, so that the embers will develop into one big flame, possibly a fire.

If you concentrate only on the bad things that you can find in yourself (even without the Gospels — it is enough to look in a mirror), then life will become a strange exercise, as if it all boils down to clearing the obstacles from a road you do not even mean to walk along. If the aim is to allow one thing or another to grow, of which you have read in the Gospels, you will inevitably bump into some form of resistance or difficulties, and then you have to combat these difficulties. But do not start by combating those difficulties that do not prevent you from being yourself, because, of course, in Scripture we can find any number of commandments that we do not fulfill, that are not natural to us. That is the asceticism accessible to any person. There is no need to be a stylite or to go into seclusion; it is enough to try to be oneself in the best Gospel meaning of the

word, following Christ's example. There is a particular spiritual
endeavor for every person.   *— Encounter, 259*

LIVING THE GOSPEL

It seems to me that the divorce between culture and religion
is largely the result of the fact that religion or, more cor-
rectly, people who practice one religion or another (and often
the Christian religion) have drastically narrowed their outlook
on things. In fact our attitude to all that is created and to
all history, culture, and learning should be the same as God's
approach — that is, a deeply rational and loving one. St. Maximus the Confessor already in the sixth century spoke of the
fact that man is created from two elements: the spiritual, which
ties him to God, and the physical, which ties him to everything
that is created in the world, and that man's task is to spiritualize
the whole of the created world and bring it to God, so that in
the words of the Apostle Paul, "God may be all in all" (1 Cor.
15:28).

Historically, it seems to me, we have in large measure forgotten this vocation of ours. On the one hand there is religion —
that is, faith, theology, people's ascetic and mystical paths —
and on the other hand it is as though the world remains outside religious thought. To say that the world is steeped in sin,
that we should not be "of this world," does not mean that we
are not responsible for everything that makes up God's created
world. And there is no aspect of this world that cannot be holy
in our eyes and rendered spiritual by a person with faith.

...Culture should be permeated with our religious experience, and should be made meaningful by it. And it seems to
me that now it is time to reappraise both our own position
and that of a culture starved of the Divine, that is, of the
secularized world.

On our own part we should repent of the fact that we have
allowed the whole world, millions of people, to lose God — in
that we proved not to be Christians to the end, that nobody

meeting us sees Christ in our eyes; our image does not reflect the shining glory of a godly life. And for this the Church as a whole, and every Christian, should repent before God.

— *Encounter,* 21

PRACTICAL CHRISTIANITY —
DEATH AND BEREAVEMENT

Metropolitan Anthony spoke often, and boldly, about death, both to Christians of all denominations and to people in the medical profession. At one time he gave annual lectures to medical students. He had met death, the dying, and bereavement in his work as a priest, as a soldier, and as a doctor, as well as among close members of his own family. His words were always, therefore, touched with personal experience.

I would like to begin by dispelling, if I can, the habitual attitude that modern men and women have developed concerning death. This is a feeling of fear and rejection, the feeling that death is the worst that can occur to a person and that at all cost survival must be achieved, even if survival has little to do with real living.

In earlier times, when Christians were nearer both to their pagan roots and to the tremendous, shaking experience of conversion, death was spoken of in terms of a birth into eternal life. It was perceived not as an end, not as the ultimate defeat, but as a beginning. Life was thought of as an ascent towards eternity, and death was felt to be that door which opens and allows us to enter it. This explains why so often the early Christians used to remind one another of death by words such as "remember death," while in the prayers that St. John Chrysostom has left us as a precious inheritance there is a petition in which we ask God to give us "a remembrance of death."

When such words are spoken to modern people, the reaction is usually one of rejection and revulsion. Do these words mean that we should remember that death is like the sword of Damocles over our heads, hanging by a hair, and that at any moment the banquet of life may end tragically? Do they mean that whenever a joy comes our way, we must be aware that it will have an end? Is it that we wish to darken the light of every day by the fear of an impending death? This is not what the early Christians felt. What they felt was that death is a decisive moment at which all that we can do on earth will have come to an end. We must therefore hurry to achieve on earth all that can be achieved. Remembering death is paradoxically an aim to achieve in life: to become the true person whom we were called by God to be, to reach as near as we can to what St. Paul calls the full stature of Christ, to become as perfectly as possible an undistorted image of God.

St. Paul in one of his epistles says that we must make haste to live because time is deceptive. We live all the days of our life as though we were writing hastily, carelessly, a draft of life that one day we will copy out in fair hand. It is as though we are just preparing to build, collecting all that will later be organized into beauty, harmony, and meaning. We live this way year after year, not doing completely, fully or perfectly, what we can do, because there is time ahead of us. We tell ourselves: later we will achieve something; later it can be done; one day the fair copy will be written. But years pass and we never do it.

This is not only because death comes, but because at every period of life we become unable to do what the previous period would have allowed us to do. It is not in our mature years that we can achieve a beautiful and meaningful youth, as it is not in old age that we can reveal to God and to the world what we might have been in our years of maturity. There is a time for all things, but once the time has gone, these things can no longer be done.

Victor Hugo said that there is fire in the eyes of the young, but there should be light in the eyes of the old. The time of the glowing fire passes, the time of light reaches us, but when the time of being a light has come, we can no longer do those things that can be done only in the days of our flaming. Time is deceptive. When we are told that we must remember death, it is not in order to give us a fear of life; it is in order to make us live with all the intensity that we could possibly have if we were aware that every moment is the only moment that we possess, and that every single moment of our life must be perfect: not a trough but the crest of a wave, not a defeat but a triumph. And so the remembrance of death seems to be the only power that makes life ultimately intense.

—*Living Orthodoxy in the Modern World*, 85

When I arrived in England I was appalled at the British attitude towards death. To die seemed to be almost an act of indecency: if you had fallen so low as to die, then there were special people who would come, undertakers, to pack and wrap you up for the funeral. Then two weeks or so later there is a nice memorial service in which one sublimates one's feelings into a kind of spiritual realm. Then I remember that I went to preach at the University Church in Cambridge on the subject of death, and a priest there told me he had never seen a dead person. Why is there this morbid attitude towards death? In a natural way one does not get rid of people through the back door! If death is nothing but defeat, the end of life, it is not pleasant for the family to look and think it will happen to them soon. Of course, if you have a wrong attitude to death, it becomes more and more horrible and frightening. I remember another incident. An old lady died, and the family telephoned me and asked me to come because I was a friend. I arrived but could see no sign of the children. I asked why they weren't there, because in the Orthodox Church the children always go to the dead person and the coffin is left open. The mother said, "They will be terrified; they know what death is." It turned out that quite recently the children had seen a dead rabbit that had been crushed by a car, and the parents thought they would be frightened if they saw granny. I asked if the children could come, otherwise, I said to the parents, they might always have this frightened attitude towards death. Eventually the parents agreed to let the children come into the house, and we went up to the room

where granny was lying. We stood beside the bed in silence for a
while, and then one of the children said, "How beautiful granny
looks." Death was no long something frightening, something to
be dreaded.   — *Beginning to Pray,* xvi

God did not create us for death and destruction; he created
us for eternal life. He called us to immortality — not only to
the immortality of the Resurrection but to an immortality that
knew no death. Death came as a result of sin. It came because
man lost God, turned away from him, looked for ways in which
he could achieve all things apart from God. The knowledge that
could have been acquired by communion with the knowledge
and wisdom of God man tried to acquire himself: instead of
living in the familiarity of God, he chose his own independence.

The French pastor Roland de Curie wrote in a way that is
perhaps a good image, that the moment man turned his back on
God and looked into the infinite in front of him, there was no
God for him, and as God is the only source of life, he could do
nothing but die. This means that there is a tragedy in death. On
the one hand, death is monstrous; death should not be there at
all. Death is the result of our loss of God. On the other hand, an
endless duration separated from God, thousands and thousands
of years of life without any hope that there will be an end to
this separateness from God, would be more horrible than the
dissolving of our bodily frame and an end of this vicious circle.

So there is another aspect of death: narrow as the gate is, it
is the only gate that allows us to escape the vicious circle of
endlessness apart from God — a creaturely endlessness in which
there is no space for our becoming again partakers of the life of
God and ultimately partakers of the divine nature. This is why
St. Paul could say: "for me to live is Christ. Death will be a
gain, because as long as I live in this body I am separated from
Christ."

This is why he said in another passage that for him to die
is not to drop from his shoulders the temporary life; for him,
to die means to be clothed in eternity. It is not an end; it is a
beginning. It is a door that opens and allows us into the vastness

of eternity that would be closed for us forever if death did not free us from our integration into earthly things.

In our attitude to death these two sides must play a role. When a person dies we can legitimately be heartbroken. We can look with horror at the fact that sin has murdered a person whom we love. We can refuse to accept death as the last word, the last event of life. We are right when we cry over the departed, because this should not be. This person was killed by evil.

On the other hand, we can rejoice, because new life, unbounded, free, has begun for him or her. And again, we can cry over ourselves, our bereavement, our loneliness, but at the same time we must learn what the Old Testament had already foreseen and foretold, when it said: "Love is as strong as death." This is the love that does not allow the memory of the beloved to fade, the love that makes us speak not in the past tense of our relationship with the beloved one: "I loved him, we were so close," but makes us think in the present tense: "I love him, we are so close."

In the New Testament, we find something even greater than this, because with the Resurrection of Christ, death is virtually overcome. Death is overcome in more than one way. It is overcome because we know through the Resurrection of Christ that death is not the last word and that we are called to rise again and to live. Death is also defeated in the victory of Christ over sin and over death itself in the harrowing of hell, because the most horrible aspect of death, as it was conceived in the Old Testament, was that the separatedness from God that had brought about death was made definitive, unconquerable, by death itself. Those who had died — and this applied to everyone — those who had died of the loss of God in death lost him forever. The Old Testament Sheol was the place where God is not, the place of definitive, irretrievable absence and separation.

In the Resurrection of Christ, in his descent into hell, in his harrowing of hell, this has come to an end. There is separation on earth and the pain of separation, but there is no separation in death from God. On the contrary, death is the moment and the way in which, however separate we were, however incompletely united or in harmony with God we were, we present ourselves before his face. God is the savior of the world. Did he not say more than once, "I have come not to judge the world but to save the world"? We stand before him who is salvation.

So death has a complexity — one could perhaps say an ambiguity — but we have no right, if we are Christ's own people, to allow ourselves to overlook the birth into eternity of the departing one because we ourselves are so deeply wounded by our bereavement and in our earthly loneliness. There is also in death a power of life that reaches out to us. If our love is faithful, if we are capable of remembering, not only with our mind but with our heart, those whom we have loved on earth, then, as Christ puts it: "where your treasure is there will your heart be also."

— *Living Orthodoxy in the Modern World*, 88

In the Orthodox Church, we bring the dead person to the church as soon as we can. We pray in the presence of an open coffin. Adults and children approach it. Death is not something to be hidden: it is something simple and a part of life. And the children can look into the face of the departed person and see the peace.

We give a kiss to the departed person. And this is the moment when we must not forget to warn the child that when he kisses the forehead of a person that was always warm, it will be cold and we can say, "this is the mark of death." Life goes with warmth. Death is cold. And then the child is not horrified, because it has experience of things cold and things warm, and each of them have their nature, and each of them have their meaning.   — *Living Orthodoxy in the Modern World*, 101

How often have we heard at the beginning of the Beatitudes the words "Remember us, O Lord, when Thou comest into Thy Kingdom!" — in the glory of Thy Kingship. . . . And these words sound so natural and simple. And yet if we imagine for one moment that when the Lord Jesus Christ comes in glory — having conquered for us and for God, overcome all evil, and made this world into his Kingdom of love, of holiness, of perfect beauty — that one of us could be forgotten: What would happen to us? Forgotten of God.... It is only because we are remembered that we exist, that we live! It is only because he remembers us even when we forget ourselves and one another that we continue to be sustained by the power of life that is his, by his blessing, by his sacrificial love.... How wonderful it is to think that we are secure in God's all-remembrance, even when people forget us!

And it happens, it happens: I remember a dark day when I was with a family, and the door opened, and a man who had been five years in the war and was thought to be dead, walked in; his wife looked at him and said, "You are alive? We thought you were dead!" And these words meant, "We counted on your death, because once you were dead, life had begun anew, in a new manner; I had met other people, I had married another man. You have come, and you should not have come; you should have remained dead."

Can you imagine what this man felt? And can you imagine what would happen to any one of us, however sinful, if, standing before God we saw that he did not remember our name, our face, our existence.... And how wonderfully inspiring it is to think that even if the whole world should forget us, there is one who will never, never forget: it is the Lord Jesus Christ, it is God One in the Trinity, God who is love.

Think of what happened in today's Gospel (Matt. 14:22–34): Peter, together with the other disciples, saw Christ as a phantom, as a ghost walking on the waters; he was filled with terror: a ghost! And they all cried out in fear. And Christ said, "Fear not! It is I!" They were tossed by the sea, as we are tossed by the circumstances of our life, by the storms that arise within us. But when they heard the voice of Christ, Peter said, "Let me come unto Thee, walking on the waters." He knew it was impossible, humanly speaking, but it was possible because all things are possible to God and in God. And Christ said, "Come!" And Peter left the frail security of the skiff in which he was with the other disciples and began to walk. And suddenly he looked at the sea instead of looking at Christ, he looked at the storm instead of looking at him who is the Lord of the storm, as he is the Prince of Peace. And because he remembered himself and the storm, he began to drown; and that very moment when he had lost sight of God, he cried "Help!" and Christ took him by the hand and brought him to shore. Here again we see that even at moments when we are carried away by our fears, by our doubts, carried away by the storm that rages within or around us, there is one who remembers in love, in compassion, in an understanding that goes beyond our own understanding. Because he has plumbed all the depths of human frailty and has carried all the weight of human sin, he can say "Fear not!" — and take us by the hand and save us. Let us think for a moment of what that means: to be remembered, and what it means to all of us, each of us that there should be people who remember us, for whom we exist, for whom we matter. A French writer has said: To say to a person, "I love you," is tantamount to saying, "You shall never die." Because it is a supreme affirmation of this person, a person who is thus affirmed cannot fall out of eternity, of God's eternity, because all love is of God. How wonderful that salvation is offered and given, how wonderful that we may be partakers of this gift, granting it to others by our love and by our eternal remembrance. Amen.

— Sermon: "Remember Us, O Lord, When Thou
Comest into Thy Kingdom," August 9, 1987

HUMILITY

When we want to know what man is, we have to look at Christ, the Christ of the Gospels, the Christ of the Mount of Olives, Christ on the cross, Christ resurrected and Son of Man seated at the right hand of the Glory of the Father. We have no need to try to make God greater by making ourselves small and contemptible. God forbids us to do so. And when we do, it is not humility that we attain but an abasement that hinders us from

living worthily of the Kingdom of God and of our human calling. How can we at one and the same time grovel at God's feet
and become sharers in the divine nature? How can we cringe
before this image of God and say: "I am a living member of
this body of which God himself in Christ is the head?" How
can we cower at the feet of God and know that we are the
Temple of the Holy Spirit, the place of his presence? Can we
regard ourselves as petty and of small account before God and
yet say, with St. Irenaeus, that in the only begotten Son, by the
Holy Spirit, we are called to be *the only begotten Son*, the *totus
Christus* and that the glory of God is man fully realized?

Humility, therefore, does not consist in forever trying to
abase ourselves and renounce the dignity that God gives us
and demands of us because we are his children not his slaves.
Humility as we see it in the saints is not born solely of their
awareness of sin, because even a sinner can bring to God a broken and contrite heart, and a word of forgiveness is enough to
blot out all evil from the past and the present. The humility
of the saints comes from the vision of the glory, the majesty,
the beauty of God. It is not even a sense of contrast that gives
birth to their humility, but the consciousness that God is so
holy, such a revelation of perfect beauty, of love so striking that
the only thing they can do in his presence is to prostrate themselves before him in an act of worship, joy, and wonder. When
the great experience of the overwhelming love that God has for
us came to St. Teresa, she was struck to her knees, weeping in
joy and wonder; when she arose she was a new person, one in
whom the realization of God's love left her "with a sense of
unpayable debt." This is humility — not humiliation.

Do we not experience a profound feeling of humility when
someone loves us — as always, quite undeservedly? We know
that love can in no wise be earned, bought, forced, obtained.
We receive it like a gift, like a miracle; there is the beginning
of humility. "God loves us for nothing," says St. Tikhon of
Zadonsk.

Humility is a way in which one stands before the face of God
who sees and man who is unaware of it; it seeks quite naturally

the lowest place as water runs spontaneously to the deepest level. It is being entirely open to God, surrendered, ready to receive from him, either from his own hand or through the mediation of other men, never proclaiming one's humble state, for it is not abasement but simply remaining before God in wonder, joy, and gratitude.

This is the only means we have of releasing ourselves from the fear of public opinion, from the subservience that frustrates our finding the courage and the opportunity to reform our lives, since we have chosen human values as our criterion. As soon as we have freed ourselves from that we are left with our conscience alone, wherein the voice of God sounds freely, declaring to us the judgment of God and enabling us to begin to live fully and in freedom. We know that we can do this because there are moments when we all break free from public opinion — moments of deep experience that make us full human beings, of true human stature, and our littleness peels off and falls away. When we are seized by great happiness, when sorrow pierces our hearts, when we are completely overcome by some inner experience, we are oblivious, if only for an instant, of what other people think of us. When we learn of the death of someone who is dearer to us than all others, we are sunk in grief; we do not ask ourselves if others look upon us favorably or not. When we meet someone we love after a long absence, we do not hesitate to throw ourselves into our friend's arms without wondering whether the crowd will think we are making fools of ourselves.   — *Meditations on a Theme*, 67

BRINGING FAITH TO THE WORLD

Metropolitan Anthony gave the following response to a question on whether an Orthodox person can learn from other cultures and faiths.

There is, of course, the obvious danger in that an inexperienced person, who has little knowledge of religion or who is intellectually unprepared, can fall under the sway of much more developed, sophisticated minds than his own and then be drawn onto some false paths.... But to read and ponder and compare everything with Orthodox teaching could be a very useful exercise in that if one does that, while continuing to pray, and continuing to live the life of the Church, one continues to meet God by every available route, that is in silence, in prayer, in reading, in the sacraments, and thus we can gradually perceive more clearly and more clearly the beauty, the depth, and the truth of Orthodoxy.

As far as the non-Christian religions are concerned, I think that nobody can *invent* God and therefore every religion that speaks about God, speaks from within some immediate experience of the Divine. This experience may be very incomplete, but it is still a real experience. It may be partly distorted by its very incompleteness, because nature does not tolerate a vacuum; but at the same time there is some direct knowledge, knowledge through experience, to which we can relate or which could open up something for us....

I do not think there is a single person in the world who has not at some time fallen on his knees before the Living God, whose presence he was suddenly aware of — or who has not met the Living God. How he will later express his experience, what forms he will give it, how he will later interpret it: this is where differences and mistakes may arise, but the root experience, it seems to me, is always real.

Of course one can say that a person can become the object of demonic temptation. But here there is a criterion by which to judge. St. Seraphim of Sarov spoke of the fact that if an inner experience is linked with light from the mind, warmth from the heart, joy, a feeling of deep humility and gratitude, then one can think that this is an experience of God. The Devil is cold: when we are under his influence we enter into darkness, coldness, arrogance and so on. If a person experiences the former, he can say that he has touched the hem of Christ's garment. I do not say that he has been in full communion with God, but his experience belongs to that which is proper to God. Of course, every time that God draws near to a person, a dark force also draws near, wanting to tear him away. As soon as you start to pray, temptations appear: as soon as you seek an integral spiritual life, immediately certain difficulties arise — both from without and from within: that is the law of everything.

Maybe I will say this to my own disgrace, but I have understood a very great deal about Christianity and about Orthodoxy through reading and consorting with non-Christians, simply with secular people, with nonbelievers, who were, if one can put it this way, "human beings"; that is, in whom I saw real people, able to love, to make sacrifices, to feel compassion, to show mercy, to be capable of everything spoken about in the parable of the sheep and the goats. In that parable there is not a single word said to suggest that people will be judged according to whether they had a belief in God; the question will be only: Were you a human being or were you less than human? If you were a human being, God's path is open to you; if you were not human, then do not presume to see heaven. And so it seems to me that everywhere one can find much that is of value — not opening oneself to everything, but looking into everything. As the Apostle Paul says: "Prove all things: hold fast that which is good" (1 Thess. 5:21). But if we do not *experience,* that is if we do not look into things, observe them, try to understand that which is outside ourselves, we will, of course, become so narrow that we will cease to be an embodiment of Orthodoxy. Because Orthodoxy is as broad as God himself. If it does not match up to God's stature, then it is just one of the religions: it is not an experience of God.   — *Encounter,* 26

ORTHODOXY

The word "Orthodoxy" is a Greek word, and it has two sides to it: it is both right glorification of God and right faith in him, and the first thing that we would say is glorification in worship. God is not someone about whom one can have notions, God is someone whom one encounters, and the English word "God" if you look it up in an etymological dictionary, proceeds from a Gothic root that means "one before whom one prostrates in adoration." So this is the first and basic sense that an Orthodox has of God: it is the one whom one meets and the one before whom one bows down in adoration. The first part of my sentence, "the one whom one meets," is a very important one because we speak very often in all denominations, in all forms of religion, of the tenets of our faith, but the tenets of our faith are the expression of people's experience, and it is not enough for a person to adhere to a world outlook or to a theology or to dogma to have a right to call himself either a Christian or a member of any other religious body. One has got a right to say, I am this and that, when it corresponds to one's personal experience, when one can say, as an atheist put it in France in a book in which he described his conversion, God exists, I have met him. This is, I think, an essential. . . .

And yet formulas play a role because formulas, or the various ways in which a faith can be conveyed, are in the end the only way of conveying things. It is by the word that one can convey notions, even if these notions are beyond words. When we say "beauty," when we say "God," when we say "love," we use words, which in themselves are empty of meaning except for one who knows what it is about. It is impossible to convey in words the substance of things. Words are signs. And in that respect the doctrinal statements of every faith including Orthodoxy are attempts at putting into words what are beyond words, or rather they are attempts at using words that will be openings and allow people to enter into an experience. I have mentioned beauty, I have mentioned God, I have mentioned love. Unless we have a slightest inkling of what these things are, the words remain meaningless but the moment we have begun to discover the thing, then the words can be used for a deeper understanding in order to share the experience of others, thereby widening our own experience.

It is not only by words that one can convey one's faith. There is an old saying that no one can abandon the world and choose for God who has not seen on the face or in the eyes of at least one person the shining of eternal life. It is because one meets someone who arrests one's attention that one can say: there is something beyond what I have known hitherto.

But there are other ways in which meaning reaches us apart from words, as I have already said: icons, you have them on the wall, are ways in which our faith can be conveyed. St. John of Damascus in the eighth century says, "If an illiterate person comes and says, 'Tell me what the Christian faith is about,' take him to the church, place him before an icon screen, and let him look." And he will see several kinds of things. Well, place him before a screen is what he said. Now I am going to comment on it. I don't want to charge poor St. John of Damascus with what I will say now. What you will see are icons, representing Christ, the Mother of God, saints, but also scenes taken from the Gospel: the Nativity of Christ, the Presentation in the Temple, and so forth. And for an illiterate person this is language, it is a way of letting him see what these events are. Having been confronted with the image, he can remember the event. On the other hand if you look at icons, you will see that they are not realistic pictures. Well, certain elements are realistic obviously. When we see the entrance of Christ into Jerusalem, if the icon is not really too bad, you are aware that Christ is riding a donkey and not a camel. So to that extent there is realism, but the aim of it is not to present a realistic picture in the sense in which we speak of realism in literature or in painting.

An icon is there to use the forms of this world, the visible elements of this world to convey meaning and not only adventures or events. So that all that is meaningful will be emphasized, all that is common ground will be just indicated. And some things will appear very strange to you. I don't know whether there are any of these icons on the wall but on a number of icons, well, you see buildings. And most of the buildings are very strange indeed. Say a house stands on two columns, a third one hanging in thin air as it were, and for a long time people used to say, How unrealistic these artists were, how primitive. Couldn't they really put the last column on something solid? Isn't it absurd?

But the idea of it was to indicate that all the things of this created world are just balanced unsafely, that it is not an order that is immutable, solid; it is not even a solid background for the life of the world. It is a transient world that one day will be either fulfilled or collapse but not a world that is self-sufficient and solidly established in itself. Now, if you turn to the faces, then you will discover other things in the same line. First of all you will discover that all icons represent personages, Christ, the Mother of God, angels, saints, facing you, never simply looking away from you because the purpose of an icon is an encounter, and one does not encounter a person otherwise than by being able to look into the face and into the eyes of that person. One does not encounter persons in profile. On the other hand, if you are prepared to look into a person's eyes, you must be prepared also to be seen, for the other person to look into your eyes, and it is an enormous risk; it's something very frightening at times, to disclose oneself so completely because one longs to look into the depth of a person's soul.

An icon is a call to all of us, to the person who contemplates it to look deeply into the presence, into the presence of a saint, of Christ, of the Mother of God, of an angel. And if you look at certain icons you will discover that when demons are represented, they are always represented in profile, because it is felt that you cannot look into the emptiness, the devastated emptiness of the demon's eyes, and remain safe.

Now, as far as faces are concerned, it is obvious that icons with a very few exceptions are not portraits. We have no portrait of Christ, of the Mother of God, of most of the saints. A few are nearing a portrait because the saints are contemporary to the artist, but on the whole the aim of an icon is not to be a portrait. The aim of an icon is to convey an experience and not simply a historical fact. If you look at the icons of the Mother of God or of Christ, they are all painted according to the same principle as caricatures. You know what caricatures are made of: one singles out a few significant features and the rest is left alone because obviously everyone knows that people have got cheeks and other parts of the face. But what is important is the eyes, the brow, the mouth, or this and that. Those of you who may remember the caricatures of de Gaulle will remember that what mattered was his nose. Well, this is the same principle that is applied in painting icons except obviously that the aim is not to make fun of the visage, of the face; and the aim is to convey something that is not amusing. And so you will find on icons eyes, eyebrows, foreheads, mouth, a basic expression; and the rest is there but it is of secondary importance. So that what you meet is what is expressive of the person and not the general universal features.

Now, in this respect, an icon is also something rooted simultaneously in the personal experience of the painter and in the common experience of the members of his Church. An icon is never a personal view of how I imagine Christ. It's never an invented countenance. And there is an interesting rule given to the icon painters, that they should never copy slavishly an icon that was painted before them, but at the same time they should never invent one because you cannot invent a spiritual experience but neither can you identify with someone else's experience to the point of being what he was. And so an icon expresses a personal experience rooted in the experience of the Church. The icons of the Mother of God are practically always icons of the Mother and Child, like the Vladimir icon which you have got there, but it not true that it is only with Christ that the Mother of God is represented. She is always related to him but not always so visibly and so obviously. There is one icon now located in the south of Russia in which we see the Mother of God alone. She has the face of a peasant girl. She has lost her veil, her hair is falling right and left on her face, her gaze is fixed, her hands, the only part of her body that one can see apart from her shoulders, which are brought forward, express agony. And when you ask yourself, What? Why? — you see in the corner of the icon in very pale yellow a Crucifix. That is the agony of the Mother contemplating the death of her Son.

And so an icon is always connected with a certain number of doctrinal views. We believe the Gospel in its integrity with, perhaps, a simplicity that may surprise a certain number of people

in the West. We believe that the Lord Jesus Christ was truly God
become truly man, we believe that he was born of the Virgin,
we believe that he lived, taught, was betrayed, delivered unto
condemnation, crucified, died and rose again and ascended into
heaven. And all this is expressed in icon painting as well as in
the doctrinal statements of the Church. To us this is history,
it is certainty, there is no question about it, and to us it is a
demarcation line at which we would say, "This is Christianity,
the rest is not or it is a Christianity that is adulterated, watered
down, submitted to the fantastic judgments of people who try
to put into acceptable imagery what is beyond the very understanding that we possess." So that to us the Gospel stands, to
us the Creed stands and stands as total reality, not as symbols
and approximations. It means that a statement contains everything that is to be stated. As I said before, a statement is a door
that opens. When we use the word "God" meaning "He before
whom one falls down in adoration," we speak of an experience,
we speak of what happens to us, we do not describe God. And
already in the fourth century St. Gregory of Nazianzus said that
if we collect from the Gospel, from the Old and the New Testament everything that God has revealed about himself, if we
put together everything that the believers have experienced and
discovered about God and try to make a completely coherent
image and say, this is our God, then we have done nothing but
built an idol, because God cannot been known in his entirety
as little indeed as a person can be known in her entirety. To
us the doctrinal statements of the Church, indeed the glimpses
of Revelation that we find in the Old and the New Testaments
concerning God are like the night sky. Every glimpse is like a
star but the spaces between the stars are as important as the
stars themselves. It is the stars that give us the direction. If we
could collect together in one flaming, glowing mass all the stars
of heaven, we would have an enormous mass of fire and no
sky left and no direction. It is because God reveals himself in
a glimpse, in a moment, that we can know that much and as
much as we can receive, perceive, commune to.

And as far as icon painting is concerned, to come back to it for one moment, there is a very interesting feature in the theory of icon painting expressed by one of our greatest painters Rublev, who lived in the fourteenth century. He always painted temporal things in three-dimensional perspective, but all the things that were eternal, even on the same icon, he painted in two dimensions. His idea was that indeed you can see Christ riding into Jerusalem, you can see the disciples, you can see the people, the trees, the houses, and you can stop to examine it and to see the relief, but things divine are shown to us in a moment; it's a glimpse, and you have never time to place them into a perspective. You know, it's a little in the way in which when you look out of the window on a very dark night during a thunderstorm, and when the lightning flashes, you see things but you cannot place them, establish a rapport of distance between them. You have seen, but what is near, what is far, what is the exact shape? It is enough for you to have seen. And this is what we try to do doctrinally in our teaching and iconographically in our icon painting. We try to reduce the elements of our faith to what was stated by the Scriptures and what is experienced in worship, but we do not try to make out of our doctrinal system a sort of total natural history of the divine world. I remember having read a book by a Western theologian that starts with these words: "Theology is a science of God as ornithology is a science of birds." Well, it isn't. It's exactly what it isn't. Ornithology can catch one bird after the other, examine it, pluck it, cut it to pieces, and say everything there is about it, and if you have got a tape-recorder even record its singing. You can do nothing of the sort with God. You can have a glimpse and fall in adoration, that's all you can do about him.

And so that informs also our worship. Our worship is based first of all on two things: on the fact that the only celebrant of a sacrament in the Church is the Lord Jesus Christ and the only person who can make real the event is the Holy Spirit of God. In the beginning of the Liturgy, the Communion service, when the priest has vested, prayed, prepared the bread and the wine that will be consecrated, when he is just about to pronounce the first words of the service, the deacon comes up to him and says, "And now, it is for God to act." You have done all you could, you have prayed, you have prepared yourself in devotion and prayer, you have vested yourself, you have prepared the elements, but that this bread should become the Body of Christ, that this wine should become the Blood of Christ is something that no human agency can effect. You will pronounce words, you will make gestures, but the act will be of God, he is the only true celebrant. That is a very important thing in our attitude to the celebrations.

On the other hand, silence plays a very important role in our worship. Quite often people who come to a church of ours say, "How bored your congregation must be: they stand and stand and they don't say a word, they don't sing. Why?" If you ask a Russian about it and indeed any Orthodox, they will say, this is the most precious thing that we possess. We can come into the church and we are in the presence, and this presence is a quality of silence. You know, the French writer Georges Bernanos in one of his books presents us with a young priest who says that at a certain moment he perceived a silence that was not made of absence of noise but had density, was solid, real, and he understood that the silence was a presence. And this is a very important thing because you can perceive the presence at the heart of the silence only if you keep silent. If you stand and become aware of this silence, if you listen to the silence, then you can gradually become aware of its depth and at the core of it recognize a divine presence. We have had examples of this. I remember a teacher of small children who tried to make them understand what silence is, that it has substance, and who allowed the class to go as wild as you can imagine, know and then at a certain moment she said, "Sh-sh, listen," and everyone got quiet. And they discovered what silence was. But it's a reminiscence, you know, like the first chapters of Genesis. So that is one thing, this sense of silence and discovery.

And I remember a man who came to us perhaps ten years ago or so. He was an atheist, he was to bring a parcel to someone in the church, and he intended to come after the service because he expected no good from what was happening in the church. Unfortunately he arrived a little too early. So he sat at the back of the church and just waited. And what he told me later was that while he was waiting, he became aware of a density of silence he had never perceived in his life and of an atmosphere. So he said to himself, "Oh, well, yes, that's collective hysteria, produced by all these people praying, that is the incantation coming from the priest and the choir, this is the sort of way in which I am drugged by the incense I am not used to, it has nothing to do with anything."

Yet it bothered him and he decided to come later at the moment when there was no one in the church. So I opened the door for him; he settled in and I left him there. Later he said to me, "You know, it's extraordinary: there was no incantation, there was no incense, there was nothing, no collective hysteria, and I still felt this silence had a density, and I thought, Is that what you mean by God?" Then he had another thought. He thought all right, supposing that is God, what's the use of God if all there is to him is that he lives in this particular building and creates this atmosphere of deep silence? I need a God who will do something about me. So he decided to come and watch the people in church, and after half a year he said, "You know, I've been watching them. I don't know whether they are becoming any better but I see them changed during the service. Something happens to them; they are different from what they are in the street. I need being changed. Could you do something to integrate me?" And eventually after a couple of years he was baptized. So here is the experience of someone who came without any expectation and who discovered through the silence something important to him.

You may be interested to know how we teach our faith. Well, I could put it in a nutshell by saying, badly, because if what I have said in the beginning makes any sense to you, it is not by making children learn doctrinal formularies or formal prayers or any such thing that you make a person into a Christian or an Orthodox. He must be introduced into an experience. And an experience can be caught as one catches the flu. It is an infection; it's not something that can be conveyed in a sterile manner. So that what we expect is that in the family people should have a sense of worship. I do not mean: do special things. It's not by praying before a meal or not praying before a meal that one conveys a sense of a sacredness of the event, but I remember one of our young theologians saying, "Everything in life is an act of divine love, even the food that we eat, is divine love that has become edible." And if the food is prepared with love, if it is served with beauty, if it is shared with reverence, if it is treated as a gift of God, it is a miracle. For people of my generation and that of my parents this attitude is easy because we have gone so often without any food and in hunger that really a piece of bread or any form of food is an act of God or an act of human love. So that is an example. The same could be applied to everything that is the life of the home — the way parents treat children and children treat parents.

I remember a scene that moved me very much. It was during the German occupation. I lived opposite a family, the family of one of our great theologians, Vladimir Lossky. I came one morning on a Sunday to fetch them to go to church, and I found the children, four of them standing side by side, and the father and the mother speaking to them and saying that they intended to make a confession and to receive communion, and they could not receive absolution from the priest and forgiveness from God if the children did not forgive them the wrongs they had done to them. And they knelt in front of each child asking for forgiveness. I remember another scene in the same family: three of the children being prepared to go to church and the fourth one not. And the fourth one said, "What about me?" "No, to go to church is a privilege. You have been so objectionable this week that you have no place there. You must first make your peace with your brothers and sister." Well, this was a lesson, I think, much more convincing than the child being taken by the arm and dragged to church while all his heart is elsewhere. He knew now that he had no place in the church because the church is a place of mutual love and there was no space for someone who had been a demonstration of carelessness and lovelessness.

Worship together with the grownups is a very important thing. One of the great things that the child discovers is that in church there is no such thing as a grownup who is always right and a child who is always wrong or wrong when everything clashes with the grownups. Everyone is a child of God, yes, but also a sinner who is in the process of salvation or otherwise, someone who stands before God exactly in the same terms whether he is as small as that or as big as anyone else. And that is a very important thing. We baptize and anoint with holy chrism the children at the same time, which means that they are full members of the Church from the very beginning, and already as babies in arms they receive communion. When they become a little bit bigger, the moment they can stand on their own feet, they are not taken by their parents to receive communion; they come individually with all the dignity they feel when they walk on their own feet and not the misery that they feel when they are taken under someone's arm and hang like this to receive communion. It's a very important thing. The sense of dignity is essential. God claims dignity from us; God is the one who respects our dignity, and the children must be taught that.

They are taught also the elements of the faith and the Gospel in a simple and natural way if the parents or the teachers are capable of conveying things. But it is a vision of a life transfigured by faith and by the real presence of God that is the convincing power. I believe that apart from this one can adhere to the tenets of one's religion, one cannot have the experience of it deeply within oneself. I can speak for myself. I never received any religious education when I was a child because my childhood coincided with the First World War, with the Russian Revolution, with years of emigration, and there was really no time and no chance with homelessness and lack of food and moving from country to country. I must say to that, really to my shame perhaps and to your pleasure, that I was not a very mystical or devout child by nature. I was taken to church once a year for Good Friday, and I discovered on my first visit to the church a wonderful thing: I discovered that if I walked into the church about three paces, breathed deeply and inhaled incense and then stopped breathing, I fainted at once and I was removed for another year from the church.

This was, I must say, my last experience of religious education.

— From a talk with Non-Orthodox, undated

2

Creation

We are ever more conscious of the necessity of preserving nature and preventing the destruction of animal and plant species, which has recently reached a frightening scale. In connection with this the word "crisis" is used. "Crisis" is a Greek word, which means, literally, judgment. A critical moment is one when all that has passed is put in question. It is very important to see a crisis as a judgment. This could be God's judgment on us. It could be Nature's judgment on us, a moment when Nature with indignation and outrage refuses to co-operate with us. It also could be that moment when we should judge ourselves — and in many cases condemn ourselves. The question as to what we have done to our earth in the last half century is placed before our conscience. The question is not one of what is profitable to us — that the earth should be fruitful and that everything in it should be at its best — but is one of our moral responsibilities before the world, created by God for love and with love, a world that he called to be in communion with him.

It goes without saying that each part of creation relates to God in an individual way, but there is no part of creation that has no relationship to God. Otherwise our understanding of the miraculous would be impossible. When Christ orders the waves to be still and the wind to cease to blow, it does not mean that he has some sort of magic power over nature, but that the living word of God is apprehended in some way by all of his creation.

Apart from the concept of judgment contained in the word "crisis," there is another understanding of it that I heard recently. The same word in Chinese means "a revealed opportunity," and that is very important. Judgment speaks of the past; but when you have come to a judgment of your own value and of the situation in which you find yourself, when you have pronounced judgment on yourself, the next step is to go forward, and not only keep looking back. That is why indeed at the moment of judgment a person probes deeply into his conscience, looking at what he has done — both personally, and collectively as a member of the human race — and thinks further as to how he should proceed. And at the moment when we begin to think of the future, we speak of what is possible. We have not yet got to the point from where there is no going back or any way forward. When there is neither any path back into the past nor a way forward, it will be the end of the world. We have not yet got to that point. But we are all responsible for something in Nature, in which we live; we all poison the earth, poison the air, we all play a part in the destruction of that which God has created. And therefore we should think about the relationship between God, the world created by him, and man.

The first thing that is clear from the Scriptures is that everything that exists was created by God. That means that by the power of his Word he called into life everything that previously did not exist. Besides, he called it all to life in order to bestow on everything and to bring everything into a state of blessedness and perfection. If one can express oneself in this way, at the moment that he was creating man and the other creatures, he was creating them out of love, he was creating them in order to share with them all the riches that belonged to him — and more than that: not only the riches that belonged to him, but even himself. We know from the Epistle of the Apostle Peter that our human vocation (we will think later about how it reflects on the rest of creation) is not only to know God, not only to bow down before him, not only to love him, but finally to become "partakers of the divine nature" (2 Pet. 1:4): that is, precisely to unite with God in such a way that God's nature should be grafted into us, so that we should become like Christ in this sense.

...I want to draw your attention to some moments in the story of creation as it is told in the Bible.

We read how God utters the Word, and that is the beginning of what had never happened before. Things start to happen and things are created for the very first time. First there appears light. There is a saying (not a biblical one, but Eastern) that light was born from the word. This is a wonderful picture: God pronounces the creative word, and suddenly light shines forth, which appears already to mark the beginning of reality. Later we see that other forms of life are formed by the order of God, step by step growing to perfection, and we arrive at the moment when man is created. It would seem that man appears as the peak of creation (and this is indeed seen both in the Scriptures and even in the simplest worldly experience). But the story of the creation of man is very interesting. We are not told that God, having created the most highly developed animals, moves on to the next step in order to create an even more complete living creature. We are told that when all creatures have been created, God takes up some wet earth and makes man out of this mud. I do not want to say that this is a literal description of what happened, but that by this we are shown that man is made from the same basic material as the whole of creation. It follows that from the same substance other creatures are also created, but it is here underlined that man is not different from other creatures, that he is, as it were, at the root of the existence of all creation, that he is created from the same elementary, basic material from which all the rest of creation has come. That somehow makes us kin, not only — as a nonbeliever would say — "the highest form of the animal kingdom," but kin to the lowest forms of life on earth. We are formed from the same material. And this is very important, because, being kin to the whole of creation, we have a direct link with all of it. And when St. Maximus the Confessor contemplates man's vocation he writes that man is created of elements of the material world and of elements of the spiritual world, that he belongs both to the spiritual world and to the material world, and he underlines that because of this, containing within himself both matter and spirit, man can bring all that is created to spirituality and bring them to God. That is man's basic vocation.   *—Encounter,* 125

The creation of man and the world is very often taken simply as an objective fact. It appears doubtful for some people and absolute for others. For some people of our time the whole theme of creation raises problems and arouses doubts, but I have very rarely met people who have thought through the theme of creation from the point of view of a living religious experience: from the point of view of what creation opens up in our relationship with God, and how it defines very deep and precious facts about the relationship of created beings to God and their relationships between themselves.

To start with I want to draw your attention to two things. First, we are not simply created, objectively, as though we were objects. We are created straightaway, even before we begin to exist, in some sort of relationship with God. God has made us because he wants us, in the warmest and deepest meaning of the word "wants." We are not necessary to God in order for him to be God. There is no necessity to call us out from nonexistence. He would be as fully a self-sufficient being, with the same fullness of exultant, joyful life, whether we existed or not. He has created us for our sakes, not for his own. And in the harmony that existed before time began, which called us into being, there already exists God's love for us in all its fullness. In his autobiography, Archpriest Avvakum speaks of this harmony before time began. God says to his Son, "My Son, let us create man!" and the Son replies, "Yes, Father!" Then, revealing the future mystery, the Father says, "Yes, but man will sin and fall away from his calling, and his glory, and You will have to redeem him on the cross," And the Son says, "So be it."

There is something very important here. It is important that God, in creating man, knew what would happen — and still he created him. He knew what would happen to man: he knew that death, suffering, and the infinite sorrow of the Fall would come to him. And he also knew that his love for man has within it the shadow of the cross, that in love there is the joy of giving and the joy of receiving, and there is the triumphant, tragic joy of the cross.

So God creates man against this background. Before man is created he is already loved by God's love on the cross, and not just by a love that is joyful and full of light. When man comes from nonbeing into being, he encounters God's love: he is loved and he is desired.

As I have already said, the creation of the world and in particular of man is not a necessity for God. It is an act of regal, creative freedom. And the fact that we are not necessary to God is the basis of a relative but nonetheless genuine originality in our being. If we were necessary to God, if without us, without creation, God would not possess the fullness of being that he has, we would be only a pathetic shadow in that shining glory; we would be like fireflies in bright sunlight. It is true we would burn with some sort of light, but in comparison to unfading Light, the shining of the Sun of truth, the midday light of Godhead, we would be limited and insignificant. It is precisely because we are not necessary to God that we have some sort of individuality. We are placed before the Face of God with some sort of independence. There can be dialogue between us and him. God spoke, and the prophets replied. A man prays, and God responds. This is possible only because we are different from God, because we do not merge with him, because man's final vocation is to become a "partaker of the divine nature" (2 Pet. 1:4) — which is not a given quality, but precisely a vocation that can be attained by gradually growing into it.

The Scriptures teach us that we are created out of nothing: from nonexistence we are called into existence. In this lies, on the one hand, our infinite poverty, and on the other, our infinitely joyful wealth. Poverty because we do not possess anything, because we are not rooted in anything. (I am now talking not only of man but of the whole of creation.) We are not rooted in God: we are deeply different from him. Neither are we rooted in anything that existed before us. According to the words of Metropolitan Filaret of Moscow, we hang between two abysses: between the abyss of nonexistence and the divine abyss, only because of God's word and will. In fact we are totally groundless, and we can obtain roots only if we become totally ourselves and akin to God, communicants of God's nature, living members of Christ's Body, temples of the Holy Spirit, the Father's children through communion — that is, all of us together in the Church, and each one of us a living member of this Church. Each one of us but not separately, because it is exactly here that one cannot use the word "separately." There is no separation between us. There is an all-conquering unity in Christ and the Spirit, so that "our life is hid with Christ in God" (Col. 3:3).

That is our calling. While we stand before the Face of God, we are called to exist. Before us lie vast expanses, and we possess nothing. That is the beginning of the Kingdom of God. Call to mind the first commandment of the Beatitudes: "Blessed are the poor in spirit: for theirs is the Kingdom of heaven" (Matt. 5:3). What sort of poverty is this that makes us members, citizens, children of the heavenly Kingdom? Of course it is not the simple, bare, and, for many, bitter fact of our total, infinite wretchedness and dependence. Spiritual poverty does not lie in this: it is the poverty that can be spiritual or can be terrible wretchedness. Remember the words of John Chrysostom, who teaches us that it is not the man who has nothing that is poor, but the man who wants to have that which he has not got. One can have nothing and not be poor: one can be rich from the point of view of everyone who looks at our lives, and feel oneself to be a wretched pauper. We are rich only, then, when we absorb everything given to us in life as God's gift and the richness of God's love.

There is a story quoted by Martin Buber that tells how in the eighteenth century there lived a rabbi in Poland. He lived in extreme, desperate poverty, and every day he gave thanks to God for all his generous gifts. Once somebody asked, "How can you thank God day after day, when you know, and know for sure, know in your flesh and in your soul, that he has not given you anything — how can you lie in prayer?" The rabbi looked at him smiling and said, "You do not understand the crux of the matter! God looked at my soul and he saw that in order that I should grow to my full stature, I need poverty, hunger, cold, and abandonment; and in this way he enriched me infinitely."

This is a marvelous story, because we see in it a man who is able to believe God and love him, and to understand God's wisdom through love, which is incomprehensible to the mind of the flesh. We see how this man in his utter wretchedness was rich — was, in a certain sense, already in the Kingdom of God.

This Kingdom of God opens to us if we understand that we radically and absolutely do not possess anything. We are, after all, called out of a state of nonexistence. We have no roots in anything, neither in God nor in anything created that preceded our creation. The life that we possess is also God's gift. We cannot create it, we cannot defend it, we cannot preserve it or keep hold of it. Our body is not in our power. It is enough for a small vein to break in our head for the greatest mind to fade and for a person to become less than an animal. It happens that sorrow and need stand before us and with all our strength we would like to feel compassion, but our heart lies in our bosom like a stone. We cannot arouse in ourselves a living feeling if it is not given to us from above. As for our will — it is unnecessary to speak of it — what can we make of ourselves? We have no power over ourselves: laziness, depression, tiredness, the circumstances of life — these are enough to break down even the strongest will. If we look around further: human relationships, kinship, friendship, love, the achievements of life, comfort, security — we have all that, and we have nothing, because we cannot hold on to anything.

How would we not grasp at all this that flows between our fingers? Everything that we possess can be taken away in an instant. And if we will think about this we will already receive some conception of our poverty, but it will be far from complete. Such a conception does not bring man into the Kingdom of God. He can fall into despair, fear, uncertainty, but still not attain that stability characteristic of the Kingdom of God, nor the joy of the Gospels. In order to enter into that joy, one has to understand something else.

We must notice first of all that with all our definitive poverty we are not in fact all that unfortunate. We do not possess either life or being, nothing in fact — and yet we have all these things. It is only philosophically speaking that we do not have them. We are alive, we move, we love, we think, we rejoice, we suffer, to speak of nothing else. But here one has to understand, to understand with both our hearts and our minds, that everything that we have is a sign of God's love at every moment, and at every hour of our lives. If we could take possession of something, it would become ours, but we would lose our link with God, which exists precisely because everything that we have is not ours but God's. All that we possess is God's love made concrete, his living care for us.

If we understand this, then indeed God's Kingdom opens up before us, because we find ourselves in this Kingdom, where above everyone and everything is God himself, who reigns eternally. He gives gifts in various ways. There are obvious blessings, and there are secret blessings, and the story of the rabbi relates to the secret blessings, blessings that few of us are capable of understanding.

That is our basic situation in relationship to God. That is what, in nonphilosophical terms, is the active life, a living, simple human experience of existence: the fact that we are created out of nothing, called into existence out of nonexistence. Within this lies our loving relationship with God, our immeasurable, wonderful richness in God. Let us remember the words in the Gospels, that the rich man will lose everything that "is not rich towards God" (Luke 12:21). That is exactly the way we *can* be rich: and we *are* rich exactly in this way. And this relationship is not a mechanical one, but a living, dynamic and moral one, having an inner, living, and spiritual content. Because the very fact that we stand before God, face to face in absolute dependence, and at the same time are endowed with the terrible power of repudiating God, of denying God, opens up before us the theme of our freedom.   — *Encounter,* 71

In popular piety, especially in the West, a tremendous amount of attention is given to mankind and the human, incarnate side of God as man. It is absolutely natural that the feeling exists that — speaking in a very simplified way — in becoming incarnate God thus became comprehensible. That is not more simplistic than what many of our believers think and feel: that God having become man, he is totally here, the infant of Bethlehem, "for in him dwelleth all the fullness of the Godhead bodily" (Col. 2:9). There is a God, and I can see him, I can embrace him. He is here; he is comprehensible. This does indeed seem so to people, and one must put them on their guard concerning it. Yes, it is true: in the Incarnation God became flesh. It is true that the incomprehensible God lived among us and "took upon himself the form of a servant" (Phil. 2:7) — but not only that. In the Incarnation something more incomprehensible is revealed than an imagined transcendental God, whom we can invent.

It may be possible to invent a heavenly God, a God whom we could characterize as having all the best human characteristics and qualities, infinitely multiplied. In his day Voltaire wrote that if there was no God, man would have to invent him. And indeed if our God displayed only infinitely multiplied human characteristics, he would be all powerful, he would be wise, he would be kind, and so on. But God as he is revealed in the Incarnation is impossible to invent, because no one would begin to invest God with qualities of which one would be ashamed: a God who is vulnerable, a God who is defeated, a God who is humiliated, a God who is condemned by a human court, who is slapped across the cheeks, a God who displays some incomprehensible weakness and unfathomable helplessness. Such a God no one could invent, and no one would. If one is going to invent a God, he must be a support, an ideal, who would be one that in time of need people would turn to with certainty that he would help, that he would stand like a wall between them and sorrow or danger or need.

Such a God who becomes a man, such a God who takes on himself the total defenselessness, the total weakness, the total vulnerability, the total apparent defeat of a man, could only be "invented" (if one can express oneself in this way) by God himself, could be presented only by God. In this sense, Christianity is more invulnerable in its faith in God than any other religion. The Christian God demands of us the very opposite of what we would like to receive from him, and for which we naturally strive. Take the Beatitudes: Blessed are those who in one way or another are unhappy — that is not what a normal person seeks for. I once gave a lecture on the Beatitudes and a very conscientious man said to me, "Your Grace, if that is the blessedness which Christians seek, please be blessed in your own way, but I want nothing of it." A normal person does not wish for such blessedness, and a normal man does not wish for such a God. And it is only because God showed himself to be like that, that we are able to know him to be such. Man would not wish to invent such a God.

Thus, in every one of God's revelations, as in this one, something is revealed about God that is incomprehensible, unfathomable. In other words, God allows us to know something that we can catch hold of, that we can grasp, that we can understand about God. And at the same time, because we have grasped something, an abyss of incomprehension opens before us that passes all understanding, that is so marvelous, so wonderful as to be overwhelming, before which we can only stand in silence and in amazement, with a trembling heart.

— Encounter, 82

HEALING

Because the Orthodox Church sees the whole person, body and soul, as good and loved by God, it lays great stress on healing, both spiritual and physical. The following selections — the first from a talk given at Metropolitan Anthony's cathedral, the second a sermon — should be read remembering that he was a medical doctor who for ten years had played his part in healing the physically sick and comforting the dying. He was not, therefore, speaking from an abstract or theological perspective, but from a very practical one. The third piece is an account of his dealing, as a priest, with a sick parishioner, in which all that he says in the first two selections come together.

There are many passages in the Gospel in which Christ, turning to a person who is sick in either mind or in body, asks a question, and this question is always: Dost thou wish to be made whole? And I think this phrase is important because it implies something that is vaster, more complete than simply restoration of health: a return to the condition that was the sick person's before illness attacked him. Because very often illness is the result of the way of life we lead, of our folly; it is the result of heredity, it is the result of outer conditions; and this is all within the compass of our situation in a world that, from a Christian point of view, is a fallen world, or if you prefer another term, a distorted world, a world that has lost its harmony, its wholeness, or has not attained it. Whatever way you look at it our world is a broken one.

A thing that has been striking me quite a lot in recent years is this: Why does Christ ask a person, Do you want to be made whole? Isn't it obvious that anyone who is sane will say: Of course I do — with the emphasis, perhaps, on the words "of course." Why are you asking a silly question? Who wishes to be ill? And yet, I think, it is a very important question, because in terms of the Gospel, to be made whole means not simply getting rid of one's physical illness, but being reintegrated to a quality of life that one did not possess before and that may be given to us on condition — the condition that being made whole, being restored to health even physically, means that we must take responsibility for our bodily and mental condition in a way in which we didn't do it before. To be healed physically is perhaps a small image of being restored to life, having come to the brink of death. The life that would have continued within us without this healing act of God would have been a life that gradually deteriorated more and more and would bring us to dying, a gradual disintegration either of our mental condition or of our physical condition. And if we are given back a wholeness that we had lost or perhaps that we never possessed before, it means that the life that is ours now after healing is not simply for us to use any way we choose. It is a gift; it is not ours in a way. We were dead, we were dying, we are brought back to a plenitude of life and this plenitude is not ours; it is a gift. So that in terms of the Gospel, as far as I can see it, when Christ says: "Dost thou wish to be made whole?" He implies: "Supposing I do it, are you prepared to lead a life of wholeness or do you want me to make you whole in order to go back to what destroyed this wholeness, destroyed you in body and soul?" And this is a question that stands before each patient, although most patients, practically all patients have no idea of the question, and it stands certainly in front of each of us when we want to be healed beyond our physical illness.

There is another aspect of wholeness restored in other situations in the Gospel when Christ says to someone: "Go and sin no more." I think we must realize that when we speak of healing in Christian terms, we do not speak simply of a power possessed by God or by his saints or by people who being neither saints nor God are possessed of a natural gift to restore health for us to continue to live in the way in which we lived before, to remain the same unchanged. God does not heal us in order that we should go back to our sinful condition. He offers us newness of life, not the old life that we have already lost. And the new life offered us is no longer ours in a way; it is his, it's a gift of his, a present. It was Mine to give, take it. And thinking in spiritual terms, it is true. Because what is sin? We define sin all the time as moral infringement, but it is much more than this: it is the very thing of which I was speaking; it is the lack of wholeness. I am divided: mind against heart, heart against will, body against all the rest. We are all not only schizophrenic, but schizo-everything, we are just like a broken mirror and so that is the condition of sin: it is not so much that the mirror doesn't reflect well; it is the fact that it is broken that is the problem. You can, of course, try to take a small piece of it and see what you can see, but it is still a broken mirror. And this brokenness of ours within corresponds to a brokenness in our relationships with other people. We are afraid of them, we are envious of them, we are greedy, what not. So it creates a whole relational sinfulness and indeed it applies supremely to God because it all results from our having lost our harmony with God. The saints are people who are in harmony with him, nothing more, nothing less, simply that. And as the result of being in harmony with God, then they can be in harmony within themselves and with other people.

And then I want to suggest something that you may find difficult to take: then in a way whether one is healed physically or not becomes a secondary thing, not to our relatives, not to our friends, but to the person concerned. What matters is the wholeness restored; and once the wholeness is restored, if together with it goes a physical healing — good; if it doesn't, it may be as good.   — From a talk on healing, November 25, 1987

Some thirty years ago a man was taken into hospital with, as it seemed, a common illness. On examination, it was discovered that he was ill with an inoperable cancer. His sister was told and so was I, but he was not. He was vigorous, strong, and intensely alive.

He said to me, "I have so much to do, and here am I, bedridden and for how long?"

I said to him, "How often you have told me that you dream of being able to stop time so that you can be instead of doing. You have never done it. God has done it for you. Now is your time to be."

Confronted with the necessity of being, in what one might call a totally contemplative situation, he was puzzled and said: "What shall I do?"

I said to him that illness and death are conditioned not only by physiological changes — by germs and pathology — but also by all those things that destroy our inner energies. This is what one may call our negative thoughts and feelings, everything that saps the power of life within us, everything that prevents life from gushing like a torrent that is clear and free. I suggested that he should put right not only outwardly but within himself all that was wrong in his relationships with people, with himself, in the circumstances of his life, and to begin in the present moment. And when he had done it in the present, to go back and ever further back into the past, clearing it all, making his peace with everyone and everything, undoing every knot, facing every evil, coming to terms in repentance, in acceptance, in gratitude, with his whole life — and his life had been hard.

So day after day, month after month, we went through this process. He made his peace with the totality of life. And I remember him at the end of it lying in his bed too weak to use a spoon, and saying to me with shining eyes: "My body is almost dead, and yet I have never felt so intensely alive as I feel now." He had discovered that life was not his body, although his body was him, and that he had a reality that the death of his body could not destroy.

This is a very important experience. It is something that we must do in the course of all our life, all the time, if we want to be aware of the power of eternal life within us and, therefore, not be afraid whatever happens to the temporary life that is also ours.   — *Living Orthodoxy in the Modern World*, 95

GENESIS

Metropolitan Anthony spoke often on the opening chapters of the Book of Genesis. In the following selections from a talk he gave at his cathedral, he speaks of the creation of man, and of woman.

I want to present you the case for the views of the Fathers of the Church on certain passages of these first three chapters of Genesis.

The words spoken by God when he created man were: "Let us make man in our image, after our likeness." And the ancient writers, as ever since, both theologians and divines, have tried to reflect deeply on two things: the difference there is between image and likeness on the one hand, and what this image of God in man is. The difference that they see is that the image is something given immediately to man at the inception of his existence. The likeness is something to be achieved, and the analogy that I think I have suggested after the Fathers is that the image can coincide with the infancy of mankind, with innocence, while the likeness is a maturity; the likeness consists in a becoming what Christ was in his incarnate days and forever remains in eternity.

If we ask ourselves further questions about the image, many visions have been suggested, but the one that impresses me particularly is the thought of St. Gregory Palamas, that what makes us akin to God is creativeness. All other beings called into existence by God are what they are. They may change in the process of time, they may improve, but they have not got within themselves the creativeness that is founded on a choice, a vision, a purpose, a motion towards a goal, and man can have this creativeness, even if the goal is wrong, even if the purpose is mistaken, even if the ways in which it is attempted are not those that will bring man to its fulfillment. Every human has that in himself.

Creativeness, however, is something more complex than the ability to call out new forms, to shape one's surroundings or even to determine to a certain extent, greater or smaller, our destiny. It begins with the ability to change — to change intentionally. Creativeness begins with the ability a being has, a human being in the given case, to become what he is not yet, to start at the point at which he was created and then grow into a fullness that he did not possess before: from image to likeness, if you will — having begun to be, as it were, a reflection, to become the reality itself; having begun to be in the image of the invisible Creator, to become in the image of God incarnate. And in this process of becoming, and this is essential in the teaching of St. Gregory Palamas, in this process of becoming, man must grow from his psychosomatic condition of being a being of body and soul to become a being of the spirit. St. Paul puts it in short when he says the first man was earthen; the last is spirit.

I think it is very important to realize that our vocation is that very thing, and when God breathes his breath into man, he did not simply give him life, because all other beings created before him were alive, but not filled with the breath of God. What this breath of God is, no one of the writers to my knowledge has ever defined in any satisfactory manner, but it is something that God has breathed into man so that man is launched on this endless motion from earth to heaven, from being of the earth to being of the spirit. And this process is a creative process. It is not an organic one; it is not something that must develop inevitably; it is something that we must choose and that we must achieve with the grace of God that is manifested, that deploys itself in our frailty, in our weakness. But this applies only to us, and however essential it is — because we move forward, Godwards, into God, into perfect communion with him so that we become in the end "partakers of the divine nature," — this would affect us only. Yet our vocation is to be the leaders of all creation into the realm of the spirit, so that gradually, in a way we cannot even fathom, all things, freed from the fetters that man's sin has imposed upon them, may grow into perfect freedom, a perfect relationship in love and worship to God, loved by God who gives himself to them, so that in the end, and again it is a phrase of St. Paul, God should become all in all.

So that here, creativeness does not apply to art, to music, to architecture, to literature, to all those things that we feel require the creativeness of mankind, both of heart and intelligence, of skill and of hand, but is much more essential and also much more important because all the rest can flow from this basic source of creativeness but cannot derive from anything else. So that here we are confronted with man, whom God has called and loved into existence, endowed with his image, launched into life, and when on the seventh day the Lord rested from his works, the seventh day will be seen as all the span of time that extends from the last act of creation on the part of God to the

last day, the eighth day, the coming of the Lord, when all things will be fulfilled, all things will come to an end, reach their goal, and blossom out in glory. It is within this seventh day, which is the whole span of history, that the creativeness of man is to find its scope and its place. And this is a wonderful call to us because each of us can be a creator within his own realm, within his mind and his soul, by making them pure and transparent to God, within his actions and life, and become what Christ said we are called to be: a light to the world, a light that dispels darkness, a light that, as in the beginning of creation is the beginning of a new day — that is, the beginning of true newness and a new unfolding of the potentialities that are within us and around us.   — The second talk on Genesis
given at the cathedral, June 1986

THE CREATION OF WOMAN

In the first chapter of Genesis we are told that man was created; man understood as a human being, not as a male, was created male and female. Some of the Fathers, following this logic of the image and the likeness, speak of the fact that man, that is, the human being created in the first place, was neither male nor female in the full sense in which we understand these words now, but was a being of still indeterminate sex, a human being containing within himself all the possibilities of male and female being. They were not in conflict, not developed so that they were side by side, but as we see them in an embryo or in the very early stages of development of a child, so that within the same being there was this bipolarity, complementary and not in opposition with one another. It is later that we discover the creation of Eve out of Adam, and the context is interesting.

The Lord, out of the ground, "formed every beast of the field, every fowl of the air and brought them to Adam to see what he would call them, and whatsoever Adam called every living creature, that was the name thereof. And Adam gave names to all cattle and to the fowl of the air and to every beast in the

field, but for Adam there was not found an help meet for him."
So that — "the Lord calls a deep sleep to fall upon Adam, and
he slept. And he took one of his ribs and closed up the flesh
thereof, and the rib which the Lord God had taken from man
made he a woman and brought her unto man." This passage,
in the context that I have mentioned, has a peculiar interest
because we see this creature that contains within himself —
as did the primeval chaos out of which all things emerge —
this bipolarity of male and female; he is the total man, in a
way, and yet not, because he is only in the incipient state that
must develop into a fullness that cannot be contained within
one unique being. It is man himself who must make the discovery, and God brings to him all his creatures, and to each
of them man gives a name, and in each of them he sees male
and female beings; and he alone stands lonely without a companion. And it is only when he discovers his aloneness, only
when he discovers that there is no one like him, that within him
there is too much and yet enough, that God calls out of this
complex human chaos of pure, innocent, and yet incomplete
potentialities a companion.

We always read the passage, "and God took one of his ribs."
The Hebrew text, like several modern languages, uses a word
that can be translated either by the word "rib," which has come
into so many translations, or by the word "side," the way in
which once can say in French *côte* or *côté*, and this is really
what is indicated, if you read some of the Hebrew commen-
taries. It is not a physical rib that God takes. He divides man
into the two halves that were so far contained in harmony and
now have come to fruition and must be separated for each of
them to attain to its complex fullness. And the word that, again,
as we are on words, is used is interesting here because in a few
lines later we see that man exclaims, "This is now bone of my
bones and flesh of my flesh. She shall be called woman because
she was taken out of man." This is not as obvious, as striking, as the Hebrew text in which the words are *ish* and *isha*,
and obviously *isha* is the feminine of *ish*. One could here say,
"because I am he and woman is she" unless one plays on the

word in a slightly Scottish way and says that facing man there is a wee man instead of a woman.

But another thing worth noticing here is that we are so used to seeing Adam — for Adam there was not found a help meet for him. And this word "help" has led to the sense that woman was created as a help, as it were as a human being destined to be subservient and helpful. This is again different from what we find in the Hebrew text, which says that there was no one capable of standing side by side, or face to face, with him.

And this notion of side by side and face to face indicates equality. It is truly the two complete halves of one being that are facing one another, and not one appointed as a help. This notion of a help was held by quite a number of ancient writers, and St. John Chrysostom puzzles for a moment over it, saying that a moment before, God had said to man that their vocation was to look after the Garden of Eden — and if that was the purpose, another man would have been much more useful for gardening purposes. So he concludes that the creation of woman was for nothing else than bearing children. This is not borne out by the text, which speaks of two beings capable of standing side by side in perfect equality before the face of God or facing one another, as we see in a moment, facing one another again, disclosing to each other something that none could see in himself.

The passage to which I refer is this: "This is bone of my bones and flesh of my flesh. She shall be called woman because she was taken out of man." They are face to face, and they look at one another and obviously Adam looking at Eve sees as it were himself, mirrored yet different. And Eve, we can assume, looks at Adam and sees herself mirrored in him, and yet different. There is at that moment something very important happening. There is a discovery by both Adam and Eve of their alterity, of the fact that they are ultimately different, that they are not simply a projection of one another or the same being in two different samples. They see one another as being the other one and yet at the same time they recognize themselves. One of the ancient writers says that at that moment, each of them could

say about the other, "This is my *alter ego*," my other myself;
and the same writer, speaking of what happens next, of the Fall
and the way in which they look at one another and see each
other naked — that is, discover something not themselves — is
the breaking up of the phrase *alter ego* into *ego* (me), and *alter*
(the other). To this, I think, we may come later.

— The second talk on Genesis
given at the cathedral, June 1986

Adam and Eve are placed in the Garden, the Garden standing
for harmony and beauty and also for becoming and blossoming
out. And in this Garden there are two trees, the role of which,
the significance of which, is important. The one is the tree of
life; the other is the tree of knowledge that reveals good and
evil. There are two ways of knowledge. The one is that which
the saints have experienced. It is the knowledge of the created
world obtained by communing with the divine knowledge: the
way in which one can see all that God has created from within
God, with his own eyes, and understand it from within God's
mind. St. Paul speaks of the necessity for us of acquiring the
mind of Christ, and the mind of Christ, I believe, is not simply
to think in Christ's own terms according to the Gospel, but
identifying with the mind of Christ, who is the Word of God,
the creative Word, the creating Word, the preserving Word and
the ultimate Savior.

Then there is another way, which consists in discovering
things on another level, of discovering things apart from God,
and apart from God one cannot see things in glory. One can see
in all things light and darkness. If you remember what I said
last time about the primeval chaos, the primeval chaos in a way
is darkness in the sense in which mystery is darkness, in the
sense in which potentialities unfulfilled, potentialities that have
not opened up into realities, are darkness; and apart from God,
when we look at things created, at history, at human beings, we
are bound to see the spark of light and the vastness of darkness. Since the Fall there is another darkness that has come into
the picture — the darkness of sin, the darkening powers of evil.

But even at the outset to look into God's creation while it is not yet perfectly unfolded and revealed confronts one with a darkness that may frighten and that may be perceived as ugliness and monstrosity in the same way in which we see a newborn baby as beautiful, but we can see an embryo as something ugly, monstrous — the difference being only that the one has not yet evolved into the harmony and perfection of the other. So do we see the whole world, ourselves, one another, history, unless we look at them from within the vision of God. And this is what the serpent offered to mankind. You need not grow into God, that requires an effort, that requires pain of growth, that requires renouncing the wonder of the present moment by moving by faith into the next moment that promises but may perhaps not lend, give what the promise holds. And the image of the serpent is a remarkably telling image.

The serpent is a being that moves only in a meandering way, never straight, always to the right, to the left, to the right, to the left, and yet aims at a goal. It's a being that cannot lift itself heavenwards but clings to the earth; even in natural history without turning to Scripture, the serpent is a being that kills.

And so here is the primeval image that the Bible gives us. The truth is straight; the way is heavenwards; the aim of all life is to give life. And here is its negation. And it is the reason why Satan expressed as the serpent is called the Murderer from the beginning, because the intention is to kill; the Liar, because it never goes straight to proclaim the truth but always meanders to blur it, and never calls us heavenwards but tries to bury us deep in the dust — "dust thou art, to dust thou shalt return."

I have said that woman was created to stand side by side, face to face, with man, both side by side looking Godwards or face to face in mutual contemplation. I don't mean narcissistic looking at one another, but a vision to see oneself and yet outside of oneself: the other myself in all the total, final otherness and yet in this perfect identity of two who really are one at the same time. When they have eaten of the tree of knowledge of good and evil, something is broken, and what is broken is that each of them looking at the other sees no longer the shining of the divine image, but sees also the incompleteness, the twilight of the darkness of what is not yet fulfilled. And at that moment, looking at one another they see themselves indeed different from one another, and they discover what the Bible calls their nakedness, because no one looking at one's own self perceives nakedness as immodesty. It is only by perceiving the other and perceiving the other in his rejection of self, in his or her ability to covet or to reject one, that nakedness is discovered. And so a tragic process occurs here. Instead of wonderful, reverent contemplation in the joy of a discovery of beauty ever growing, a beauty that ever expands into a greater perfection, of discovering that this beauty is a revelation of one's own beauty at the same time because of the oneness between the two, there is a vision of otherness, alienation. And the next step is covetousness, enslavement, and the loss of integrity and wholeness. In the beginning we see, "and they were both naked, the man and his wife, and they were not ashamed." And later we see that they knew that they were naked, and they were ashamed of one another.

The result of it was the Lord's words concerning both the created world around them and their mutual relationship. The Lord said, "Behold, the man" — that is the human being — "is become as one of us." The commentary given very often is that this phrase is a sinister and cynical joke. Become one of us to know good and evil. He tried and look at him, he knows good and evil, he imagines that he is like a person of the Holy Trinity.

What I believe is true about it, and I have no authority for it, is that it means man, who in his totality, he and she, was an image of, an incipient image of Trinitarian oneness and love, is now broken, he is no longer one, he is made of two broken halves, as though the Trinity had been broken to pieces like a mirror.   — The second talk on Genesis
given at the cathedral, June 1986

3

Prayer

Metropolitan Anthony was known, perhaps more than anything else, for his books on prayer. They were published during
the 1960s and 1970s and were taken from transcripts of public
talks he had given on the subject. These were his core books —
indeed, the only books published during his lifetime in the
English language.

It is important to note that what he said was, in the main,
intended for anyone who would listen, and not specifically for
an Orthodox audience. Indeed, the talks on which Beginning
to Pray was based were aimed expressly at nonbelievers. They
were given at Exeter College, Oxford, in 1969 as part of a
university mission, and a notice "Believers not admitted" was
posted on the door, according to Metropolitan Anthony.

Therefore most of these books are not studies in Orthodox piety, but practical suggestions for bringing the reader to
God through prayer. At other times he did speak to Orthodox
audiences, and with a more characteristically Orthodox voice.

Whatever the make-up of Metropolitan Anthony's audiences
and readers, one thing remained constant: he spoke as a Christian from the Orthodox tradition, and the Orthodox outlook
pervaded his words. This is especially obvious in what he had
to say on the Jesus Prayer.

Metropolitan Anthony's own prayer was striking. When he
celebrated the Liturgy or recited the evening prayers after his
regular talks at his cathedral, he generated a sense of prayerful

reverence that drew his listeners deeper into their own communion with God. His spiritual children felt carried by his prayer. He might, in the course of hearing a confession, retreat for a moment into inaudible but obvious prayer, before offering advice. He would sometimes — but by no means always — give a person a more or less defined rule of prayer, perhaps in conjunction with preparing for Communion. The Orthodox Church prescribes lengthy pre-Communion prayers, and a long set of prayers to be said on the morning of the Liturgy. Metropolitan Anthony might advise a person, say, to read them section by section over a number of days. His advice was always to be intelligent in one's prayer life, not to let it become mechanical, and "when a rule becomes a routine, change it."

He described his own beginnings in the life of prayer, following his conversion, in "Without Notes," a chapter in his book Encounter *(published during his lifetime in Russia and translated and published posthumously in England):*

I began to pray. Nobody taught me how to do it, so I experimented: I simply knelt down and prayed as best I could. I then came across a teaching guide to the Book of Hours, and I began to learn how to read Old Slavonic and read out the services. This took about eight hours a day, but I did not do this for long because life did not allow for it. By that time I had already entered university and it was impossible to combine this with a full university course. But then I began to learn the services by heart, and as I walked to the university and to the hospital for my clinical practice I managed to recite the morning service on the way there, and to read the Hours on the way back. I did not *set out* to read them. It was simply that it was a great pleasure for me, and therefore I read them. . . . In the evening I prayed for a long time — simply because I am very slow, and my method of praying was also very slow. In effect I read the evening prayers three times: reading over each sentence, then falling silent, reading it a second time with a full veneration — bowing to the ground — and then again for a final understanding — and this applied to the whole set of evening prayers. All this took two and a half hours, which was not always very convenient, but it was very nourishing and satisfying, because it then comes to a point when you respond with your whole body. "Lord, have mercy!" ... Through this I acquired a sense that this was life. While I was praying I was alive; without it there was something lacking, something missing.

— "Without Notes," *Encounter,* 200

Having begun his own life as a believer with a direct encounter with Christ, Metropolitan Anthony was adamant that an encounter between a person and God was central to the life of prayer; indeed, he did not envisage Christianity without it.

He understood, however, that real encounter with God was not achieved mechanically; neither was it something that should be sought lightly, for it came at a cost to the "old man" in us.

THE ABSENCE OF GOD

At the outset there is one very important problem: the situation of one for whom God seems to be absent. This is what I would like to speak about now. Obviously, I am not speaking of a real absence — God is never really absent — but of the *sense* of absence that we have. We stand before God and we shout into an empty sky, out of which there is no reply. We turn in all directions and he is not to be found. What ought we to think of this situation?

It is very important to remember that prayer is an encounter and a relationship, a relationship that is deep, and this relationship cannot be forced either on us or on God. The fact that God can make himself present or can leave us with the sense of his absence is part of this live and real relationship. If we could mechanically draw him into an encounter, force him to meet us, simply because we have chosen this moment to meet him, there would be no relationship and no encounter. We can do that with an image, with the imagination, or with the various idols we can put in front of us instead of God; we can do nothing of the sort with the living God, any more than we can do it with a living person. A relationship must begin and develop in mutual freedom. If you look at the relationship in terms of *mutual* relationship, you will see that God could complain about us a great deal more than we about him. We complain that he does not make himself present to us for the few minutes we reserve for him, but what about the twenty-three and a half hours during which God may be knocking at our door and we answer "I am busy, I am sorry." Or when we do not answer at all because we do not even hear the knock at the door of our heart, of our minds, of our conscience, of our life. So there is a situation in which we have no right to complain of the absence of God, because we are a great deal more absent than he ever is.

The second very important thing is that a meeting face to face with God is always a moment of judgment for us. We cannot meet God in prayer or in meditation or in contemplation and not be either saved or condemned. I do not mean this in major terms of eternal damnation or eternal salvation already given and received, but it is always a critical moment, a crisis. "Crisis" comes from the Greek and means "judgment." To meet God face to face in prayer is a critical moment in our lives, and thanks be to him that he does not always present himself to us when we wish to meet him, because we might not be able to endure such a meeting. Remember the many passages in Scripture in which we are told how bad it is to find oneself face to face with God, because God is power, God is truth, God is purity. Therefore, the first thought we ought to have when we do not tangibly perceive the divine presence is a thought of gratitude. God is merciful; he does not come in an untimely way. He gives us a chance to judge ourselves, to understand, and not to come into his presence at a moment when it would mean condemnation. — *Beginning to Pray*, 2

In order to be able to pray, we must be within the situation defined as the Kingdom of God. We must recognize that he is God, that he is king, we must surrender to him. We must at least be concerned with his will, even if we are not yet capable of fulfilling it. But if we are not, if we treat God like the rich young man who could not follow Christ because he was too rich, then how can we meet him? So often what we would like to have through prayer, through the deep relationship with God that we long for, is simply another period of happiness; we are not prepared to sell all that we have in order to buy the pearl of great price. Then how should we get this pearl of great price? Is that what we expect to get? Is it not the same as in human relationships: when a man or a woman experience love for another, other people no longer matter in the same way. To put it in a short formula from the ancient world, "When a man has a bride, he is no longer surrounded by men and women, but by people."

Isn't that what could, what should happen with regard to all our riches when we turn to God? Surely they should become pale and gray, just a general background against which the only figure that matters would appear in intense relief. We would like just one touch of heavenly blue in the general picture of our life, in which there are so many dark sides. God is prepared to be outside it. He is prepared to take it up completely as a cross, but he is not prepared to be simply part of our life.

So when we think of the absence of God, is it not worthwhile to ask ourselves whom we blame for it? We always blame God, we always accuse him, either straight to his face or in front of people, of being absent, of never being there when he is needed, never answering when he is addressed. At times we are more "pious" (very much in quote marks), and we say piously, "God is testing my patience, my faith, my humility." We find all sorts of ways of turning God's judgment on us into a new way of praising ourselves. We are so patient that we can put up even with God!   — *Beginning to Pray*, 5

Whenever we approach God the contrast that exists between what he is and what we are becomes dreadfully clear. We may not be aware of this as long as we live at a distance from God, so to speak, as long as his presence or his image is dimmed in our thoughts and in our perceptions; but the nearer we come to God, the sharper the contrast appears. It is not the constant thought of their sins, but the vision of the holiness of God that makes the saints aware of their own sinfulness. When we consider ourselves without the fragrant background of God's presence, sins and virtues become small and somewhat irrelevant matters; it is against the background of the divine presence that they stand out in full relief and acquire their depth and tragedy.

... Therefore, before we set out on the so-called thrilling adventure of prayer, it cannot be too strongly stated that nothing more significant, more awe-inspiring, can occur than meeting the God we set out to meet. It is essential to realize that we will lose our life in the process: the old Adam we are must die. We are intensely attached to the old man, afraid for him, and it is very difficult, not only at the outset but years after we have begun to feel that we are completely on the side of Christ, against the old Adam.

Prayer is an adventure that brings not a thrill but new responsibilities: as long as we are ignorant, nothing is asked of us, but as soon as we know anything, we are answerable for the use we make of that knowledge. It may be a gift, but we are responsible for any particle of truth we have acquired; as it becomes our own, we cannot leave it dormant but have to take it into account in our behavior, and in this sense we are to answer for any truth we have understood.

It is only with a feeling of fear, of adoration, with the utmost veneration that we can approach this adventure of prayer, and we must live up to it outwardly as completely and precisely as possible. It is not enough to lounge in an armchair, saying, Now, I place myself in an act of veneration in the presence of God. We have to realize that if Christ were standing in front of us, we would comport ourselves differently, and we must learn to behave in the presence of the invisible Lord as we would in the presence of the Lord made visible to us.

— *Living Prayer,* 11

As long as we care deeply for all the trivialities of life, we cannot hope to pray wholeheartedly; they will always color the train of our thoughts. The same is true about our daily relations with other people, which should not consist merely of gossip but should be based on what is essential in every one of us; otherwise we may find ourselves unable to reach another level when we turn to God. We must eradicate everything meaningless and trivial in ourselves and in our relations with others and concentrate on those things we shall be able to take with us into eternity.

It is not possible to become another person the moment we start to pray, but by keeping watch on one's thoughts one learns gradually to differentiate their value. It is in our daily life that we cultivate the thoughts that irrepressibly spring up at the time of prayer. Prayer in its turn will change and enrich our daily life, becoming the foundation of a new and real relationship with God and those around us.

In our struggle for prayer the emotions are almost irrelevant; what we must bring to God is a complete, firm determination to be faithful to him and strive that God should live in us. We must remember that the fruits of prayer are not this or that emotional state, but a deep change in the whole of our personality. What we aim at is to be made able to stand before God and to concentrate on his presence, all our needs being directed Godwards, and to be given power, strength, anything we need that the will of God may be fulfilled in us. That the will of God should be fulfilled in us is the only aim of prayer, and it is also the criterion of right prayers. It is not the mystical feeling we may have, or our emotions that make good praying. Theophan the Recluse says: "You ask yourself, 'Have I prayed well today?' Do not try to find out how deep your emotions were, or how much deeper you understand things divine; ask yourself: 'Am I doing God's will better than I did before?' If you are, prayer has brought its fruits, if you are not, it has not, whatever amount of understanding or feeling you may have derived from the time spent in the presence of God."

Concentration, whether in meditation or in prayer, can be achieved only by an effort of will. Our spiritual life is based on our faith and determination, and any incidental joys are a gift of God. St. Seraphim of Sarov, when asked what it was that made some people remain sinners and never make any progress while others were becoming saints and living in God, answered, "Only determination." Our activities must be determined by an act of will, which usually happens to be contrary to what we long for; this will, based on our faith, always clashes with another will, our instinctive one. There are two wills in us, one is the conscious will, possessed to a greater or lesser degree, which consists in the ability to compel ourselves to act in accordance with our convictions. The second one is something else in us; it is the longings, the claims, the desires of all our nature, quite often contrary to the first will. St. Paul speaks of two laws that fight against each other (Rom. 7:23). He speaks of the old and the new Adam in us, who are at war. We know that one must die in order that the other should live, and we must realize that our spiritual life, our life as a human being taken as a whole, will never be complete as long as these two wills do not coincide. It is not enough to aim at the victory of the good will against the evil one; the evil one, that is, the longings of our fallen nature, must absolutely, though gradually, be transformed into a longing, a craving for God. The struggle is hard and far-reaching.

The spiritual life, the Christian life, does not consist in developing a strong will capable of compelling us to do what we do not want. In a sense, of course, it is an achievement to do the right things when we really wish to do the wrong ones, but it remains a small achievement. A mature spiritual life implies that our conscious will is in accordance with the words of God and has remolded, transformed our nature so deeply, with the help of God's grace, that the totality of our human person is only one will.

We must...be prepared to do God's will and pay the cost. Unless we are prepared to pay the cost, we are wasting our time. Then, as a next step, we must learn that doing is not enough, because we must not be drilled into Christianity, but we must become Christians; we must learn, in the process of doing the will of God, to understand God's purpose. Christ has made his intention clear to us and it is not in vain that in St. John's Gospel he no longer calls us servants but friends, because the servant does not know the mind of the master, and he has told us all things (John 15:15). We must, by doing the will of God, learn what this doing implies, so that in thought, in will, in attitude, we may become co-workers with Christ (1 Cor. 3:9). Being of one mind we shall gradually become inwardly what we try to be outwardly.

We see that we cannot partake deeply of the life of God unless we change profoundly. It is therefore essential that we should go to God in order that he transform and change us, and that is why, to begin with we should ask for conversion. Conversion in Latin means a turn, a change in the direction of things. The Greek word *metanoia* means a change of mind. Conversion means that instead of spending our lives looking in all directions, we should follow one direction only. It is a turning away from a great many things that we valued solely because they were pleasant or expedient for us. The first impact of conversion is to modify our sense of values. With God being at the center of all, everything acquires a new position and a new depth. All that is God's, all that belongs to him, is positive and real. Everything that is outside him has no value or meaning.

But it is not a change of mind alone that we can call conversion. We can change our minds and go no further; what must follow is an act of will and unless our will comes into motion and is redirected Godwards, there is no conversion; at most there is only an incipient, still dormant and inactive change in us. Obviously it is not enough to look in the right direction and never move. Repentance must not be mistaken for remorse; it does not consist in feeling terribly sorry that things went wrong in the past; it is an active, positive attitude that consists in moving in the right direction. It is made very clear in the parable of the two sons (Matt. 21:28) who were commanded by their father to go to work in his vineyard. The one said, "I am going," but did not go. The other said, "I am not going," and then felt ashamed and went to work. This was real repentance, and we should never lure ourselves into imagining that to lament one's past is an act of repentance. It is part of it of course, but repentance remains unreal and barren as long as it has not led us to doing the will of the father. We have a tendency to think that it should result in fine emotions, and we are quite often satisfied with emotions instead of real, deep changes.

When we have hurt someone and realize that we were wrong, quite often we express our sorrow to the person, and when the conversation has been emotionally tense, when there were a lot of tears and forgiveness and moving words, we go away with a sense of having done everything possible. We have wept together, we are at peace, and now everything is all right. It is not all right at all. We have simply delighted in our virtues and the other person, who may be goodhearted and easily moved, has reacted to our emotional scene. But this is just what conversion is not. No one asks us to shed tears, nor to have a touching encounter with the victim, even when the victim is God. What is expected is that having understood the wrong, we should put it right.

Nor does conversion end there; it must lead us farther in the process of making us different. Conversion begins but it never ends. It is an increasing process in which we gradually become more and more what we should be, until, after the day of judgment, these categories of fall, conversion, and righteousness disappear and are replaced by new categories of a new life, As Christ says: "I make all things new" (Rev. 21:5).

— Living Prayer, 61

I don't know what happens in the mysterious way in which the soul is related to God. I believe that whoever calls on God, whatever name he gives him, speaks to the only God. If a man prays and calls on an imaginary God, it is the real God who hears. God responds to what is in the heart of men, not to their intellectual judgments or to their lack of factual knowledge. But I think that when people have discovered Christ, there is a moment when all other names must go. There is a uniqueness in Christ that cannot be set side by side with any other name. There have been great and holy teachers of humanity apart from Christ, but no one has been or ever shall be what Christ is: God who has come into this world. Not because his teaching was better than anyone else's: the point is the Person and the event of the Incarnation.   — *Our Life in God*, 45

DISCIPLESHIP

When we think of spiritual discipline, we usually think in terms of rules of life, rules of thinking and meditation, rules of prayer, which are aimed at drilling us into what we imagine to be the pattern of a real Christian life. But when we observe people who submit themselves to that kind of strict discipline, and when we ourselves attempt this, we usually see that the results are far less than we would expect. And this generally comes from the fact that we take the means for the end, that we concentrate so much on the means that we never achieve the end at all, or that we achieve it to so small a degree that it was not worth putting in all that effort to achieve so little. This results, I believe, from not understanding what spiritual discipline is and what it is aimed at.

We must remember that discipline is not the same thing as drill. Discipline is a word connected with the word "disciple." Discipline is the condition of the disciple, the situation of the disciple with regard both to his master and to what he is learning. And if we try to understand what discipleship means when it is put into action, when it results in discipline, we may easily find the following things. First of all, discipleship means a sincere desire to learn and a determination to learn at all cost. I know that the words "at all cost" may mean a great deal more for one person than for another. It depends on the zeal and the conviction or the longing we have for the learning. Yet it is always "at all cost" for this particular person. A sincere desire to learn is not so often to be discovered in our hearts. Quite often we wish to learn up to a point, provided the effort will not be too great, provided we have guarantees that the final result will be worth the effort. We do not launch into this learning wholeheartedly enough and this is why so often we do not achieve what we could achieve. So the first condition if we wish to become disciples fruitfully and learn a discipline that will give results, is integrity of purpose. This is not easily acquired. We must also be ready to pay the cost of discipleship. There is always a cost to discipleship because, from start to finish, it means a gradual overcoming of all that is self in order to grow into communion with that which is greater than self and which will ultimately displace self, conquer the ground and become the totality of life. And there is always a moment in the experience of discipleship when fear comes upon the disciple, for he sees at a certain moment that death is looming, the death that his self must face. Later on it will no longer be death; it will be a life greater than his own, but every disciple will have to die first before he comes back to life. This requires determination, courage, faith. *— Meditations on a Theme*, 14

Discipleship begins with silence and listening. When we listen to someone we think we are silent because we do not speak; but our minds continue to work, our emotions react, our will responds for or against what we hear, we may even go further than this, with thoughts and feelings buzzing in our heads that are quite unrelated to what is being said. This is not silence as it is implied in discipleship. The real silence towards which we must aim as a starting point is a complete repose of mind and heart and will, the complete silence of all there is in us, including our body, so that we may be completely aware of the word we are receiving, completely alert and yes, in complete repose. The silence I am speaking of is the silence of the sentry on duty at a critical moment: alert, immobile, poised, and yet alive to every sound, every movement. The living silence is what discipleship requires first of all, and this is not achieved without effort. It requires from us a training of our attention, a training of our body, a training of our mind and our emotions so that they are kept in check, completely and perfectly.

The aim of this silence is the perceiving of what will be offered us, of the word that will resound in the silence. And this word we must be prepared to hear, whatever it may be. This requires a moral, intellectual integrity, because very often we listen hoping that we shall hear what we wish to hear and ready at the very moment we do not hear the right words, to switch off our understanding or our attention in order not to hear; or else we switch on the sinister ability we have to misunderstand, to misinterpret, to understand in our way what is spoken in God's way. Here again training in moral and intellectual integrity is essential. Then when we listen, we shall hear; we may hear dimly or clearly, we may hear all we need to know or, to begin with, just enough for us to have a clue, to pay more attention, to learn more about silence and about listening. But in order to hear we must be prepared to receive any word that will be spoken to us, and in order to understand we must be prepared to do whatever God commands.

— *Meditations on a Theme*, 15

In the stories of the Desert Fathers there is an encounter between one of the great masters of the desert and three monks. Two of them ask him endless questions; the other remains silent. At last the father turns to him and says, "Aren't you going to ask me anything?" "No," he replies, "it is enough for me to look at you." There is another story of a bishop of Alexandria who was coming to visit a monastery. The monks invited one of the brethren to make a speech of welcome, but he refused. "Why?" they asked. "If he does not understand my silence he will not understand a thing I have to say to him."

— *Meditations on a Theme*, 72

"Prayer is the most important thing," Metropolitan Anthony would say to his spiritual children, talking to them of private prayer. This one-to-one relationship with God was, he thought, more important than attending services. But he understood that

*many people found private prayer difficult, and he was full of
very practical advice.*

In answer to the question, "Is it failure, or merely a necessary
adaptation to our fast-paced lives today, that we often don't
find the time to spend fifteen minutes or half an hour set aside
solely for prayer before work?"

"I think it is a failure of the same kind that a man would
make who said to his wife, 'I have no time for you, but I'm
earning your bread, I'm buying you presents, what else do you
want of me?' That's no relationship. Perhaps the wife would
say, 'Please, don't work additional hours in order to buy me a
new muff or a new bag, but spend this time with me.' The only
thing that is of value between God and you is the way in which
you relate."   —*Practical Prayer,* 9

Unless we can find the right name for God, we have no free,
real, joyful, open access to him. As long as we have to call
God by general terms like "The Almighty," "The Lord God,"
as long as we have got to put "the" before the word to make
it anonymous, to make it a generic term, we cannot use it as
a personal name. But there are moments when the sacred writers, for instance, burst out with something that has the quality
of a nickname, something that no one else could possibly say,
which is at the limit of the possible and the impossible, which is
made possible only because there is a relationship. Remember
the psalm in which, after more restrained forms of expression, suddenly David bursts out, "You, my joy!" That is the
moment when the whole psalm comes to life. Saying "O Thou
our Lord," "O you are the Almighty," and the like, was stating
to God facts about him, but bursting out and saying "O You my
Joy!" was quite a different thing. And when we can say to God,
"O You my Joy!" or when we can say "O You the pain of my
life, O You who are standing in the midst of it as torment, as a
problem, as a stumbling block!" when we can address him with
violence, then we have established a relationship of prayer....

I am quite certain that if some day "O You my Joy!" or any other cry of this kind bursts out of you, it will be the moment when you will have discovered a relationship between him and you that is your own, which is not a relationship that you share with many other people. I do not mean to say that you should not share it. We have words for God that belong to all of us, but there are words that belong only to me or to you in the same way in which, in human relationships, there are surnames, there are Christian names, there are nicknames. It is good if you can have a nickname by which you can call the Almighty God, a nickname that has all the depth of your heart, all the warmth you are capable of; it becomes your way of saying "In my uniqueness this is the way I perceive your uniqueness."

— Beginning to Pray, 67

Awake in the morning and the first thing you do, thank God for it, even if you don't feel particularly happy about the day to come. "This day that the Lord has made, let us rejoice and be grateful in it." Once you have done this, give yourself time to realize the truth of what you are saying and really mean it — perhaps on the level of deep conviction and not of what one might call exhilaration. And then get up, wash, clean, do whatever else you have got to do, and then come to God again. Come to God again with two convictions. The one is that you are God's own, and the other is that this day is also God's own, it is absolutely new, absolutely fresh. It has never existed before. To speak in Russian terms, it is like a vast expanse of unsoiled snow. No one has trodden on it yet. It is all virgin and pure in front of you. And now, what comes next? What comes next is that you ask God to bless this day, that everything in it should be blessed and ruled by him. After that you must take it seriously, because very often one says, "O God, bless me," and having received the blessing we act like the prodigal son — we collect all our goods and go to a strange country to lead a riotous life.

This day is blessed by God, it is God's own, and now let us go into it. You walk in this day as God's own messenger; whoever you meet, you meet in God's own way. You are there to be the presence of the Lord God, the presence of Christ, the presence of the Spirit, the presence of the Gospel — this is your function on this particular day. God has never said that when you walk into a situation in his own Name, he will be crucified and you will be the risen one. You must be prepared to walk into situations, one after the other, in God's name, to walk as the Son of God has done: in humiliation and humility, in truth and ready to be persecuted and so forth. Usually what we expect when we fulfill God's commandments is to see a marvelous result at once. We read of that at times in the lives of the saints. When, for instance, someone hits us on one cheek, we turn the other one, although we don't expect to be hit at all, but we expect to hear the other person say, "What, such humility" — you get your reward and he gets the salvation of his soul. It does not work that way. You must pay the cost and very often you get hit hard. What matters is that you are prepared for that. As to the day, if you accept that this day was blessed of God, chosen by God with his own hand, then every person you meet is a gift of God, every circumstance you will meet is a gift of God, whether it is bitter or sweet, whether you like or dislike it. It is God's gift to you and if you take it that way, then you can face any situation. But then you must face it with the readiness that anything may happen, whether you enjoy it or not, and if you walk in the name of the Lord through a day that has come fresh and new out of his own hands and has been blessed for you to live with it, then you can make prayer and life really like the two sides of one coin. You act and pray in one breath, as it were, because all the situations that follow one another require God's blessing.   — *Beginning to Pray,* 46

AN EXERCISE

Try to find time to stay alone with yourself: shut the door and settle down in your room at a moment when you have nothing else to do. Say "I am now with myself," and just sit with yourself. After an amazingly short time you will most likely feel bored. This teaches us one very useful thing. It gives us insight into the fact that if after ten minutes of being alone with ourselves we feel like that, it is no wonder that others should feel equally bored! Why is this so? It is so because we have so little to offer to our own selves as food for thought, for emotion and for life. If you watch your life carefully you will discover quite soon that we hardly ever live from within ourselves; instead we respond to incitement, to excitement. In other words, we live by reflection, by reaction. Something happens and we respond, someone speaks and we answer. But when we are left without anything that stimulates us to think, speak, or act, we realize that there is very little in us that will prompt us to action in any direction at all. This is really a very dramatic discovery. We are completely empty; we do not act from within ourselves but accept as our life a life that is actually fed in from outside; we are used to things happening that compel us to do other things. How seldom can we live simply by means of the depth and the richness we assume that there is within ourselves.

There is a passage in Dickens's *Pickwick Papers* that is a very good description of my life and probably also of your lives. Pickwick goes to the club. He hires a cab and on the way he asks innumerable questions. Among the questions, he says, "Tell me, how is it possible that such a mean and miserable horse can drive such a big and heavy cab?" The cabbie replies "It's not a question of the horse, Sir. It's a question of the wheels," and Mr. Pickwick says "What do you mean?" The cabbie answers, "You see, we have a magnificent pair of wheels which are so well oiled that it is enough for the horse to stir a little for the wheels to begin to turn and then the poor horse must run for its life." Take the way that we live most of the time. We are not the horse that pulls; we are the horse that runs away from the cab in fear of its life.

Because we don't know yet how to act without an outer reason, we discover that we don't know what to do with ourselves, and then we begin to be increasingly bored. So first of all, you

must learn to sit with yourself and to face boredom, drawing
all the possible conclusions.

After a while this becomes worse than boredom because we
are not simply bored in a way that allows us to say, "I am
an active person and am of use to my neighbor. I always do
good, and for me to be in the state of suspense where I am not
doing anything for anyone else is a severe trial." We begin to
discover something else. We are bored when we try to get out
of this boredom by turning inward to see if there is anything
in ourselves that will put an end to it. Quite soon we discover
that there is nothing, since all we have to think about we have
already thought about dozens of times. All the range of emotions that we have in store are not used to the piano playing
itself. We must have someone else playing on the keys. We are
not in the habit of doing nothing, and so it becomes worry-
ing and can lead us to the point of anguish. If you read the
Desert Fathers, who had good experience of this, or the monks
who spent their lives in monasteries, you will see that there
are moments when they simply ran out of their cells shouting
for help, trying to meet something or someone, whatever they
could find. The devil himself would have been better than this
emptiness of self-contemplation. One of the spiritual writers,
Theophan the Recluse, says "Most people are like a shaving
of wood curled around its central emptiness." If we are really
honest, we must admit that this is a very apt description of the
state of practically all of us.

Then we must be able to fight this anguish and to say "No,
I will stick it through, and I will come to the point where the
anguish itself will prompt me to do what good will is incapable
of doing." Indeed, a moment comes, a moment of despair and
anguish and terror, that makes us turn even deeper inward and
cry, "Lord have mercy! I am perishing, Lord save me!" We discover that there is nothing in us that can give life, or rather is
life; and that all we called life, imagine life to be, was outside,
and inside there was nothing.

Then we look into the abyss of nonentity and we feel that
the deeper we go into it the less there will be left of us. This

is a dangerous moment; this is the moment when we must hesitate.

At this point we have reached the first layer of depth where we begin to be able to knock at a door. For on the layer where we were just resting from our neighbor before we felt bored, on the layer where we are simply bored and feel offended that we should be, on the layer on which we begin to fidget and worry, then feel slightly anguished, we have as yet no reason to cry and shout with a despair that fills all our mind, all our hearts, all our will, and all our body with a sense that unless God comes I am lost, there is no hope, because I know that if I emerge out of this depth I will simply be back in the realm of delusion, of reflected life, but not real life.

This is the point at which we can begin to knock at a door still closed, but beyond which there is hope, that hope which Bartimaeus, the blind man at the gates of Jericho, felt, out of his utmost despair, when Christ was passing.

— *Beginning to Pray*, 38

DESPAIR AND PRAYER

We know from the Gospels that Bartimaeus found himself by the side of the road, hopelessly blind, having lost all faith and all hope in human help, and reduced to beg for his living, to hope not really on charity (the word meaning "cherishing"), but on the kind of charity that consists in throwing coins to someone without ever having seen him. And one day this man, who had now given up hope, who was installed in the dust in his present blindness, heard about the man, a new prophet, who was now working miracles throughout the Holy Land. Had he had eyes he would probably have got up and run throughout the country to find him, but he couldn't possibly keep pace with this itinerant wonderworker. And so he stayed where he was, and the presence of one who might possibly have cured him must have made his despair even greater, even more poignant. And one day he heard a crowd that passed by, a crowd which did not sound like any other crowd. Probably, as the blind do, he had developed the sense of hearing and the sensitiveness greater than ours, because he asked "who is it that passes by?" and he was told "Jesus of Nazareth." And then he stood at the point of utmost despair and of utmost hope. Utmost hope because Christ was passing within reach, but at the background the looming despair because a few paces would have brought him level with Bartimaeus, a few more paces and he had gone and would probably never pass by him again. And out of this desperate hope he began to cry and shout, "Jesus, son of David, have mercy on me." It was a perfect profession of faith. And at that moment it was because his despair was so deep that he could summon such daring hope in order to be healed, saved, made whole. And Christ heard him.

...There is a degree of despair that is linked with total, perfect hope. This is the point at which, having gone inward, we will be able to pray; and then "Lord have mercy" is quite enough. We do not need to make any of the elaborate discourses we find in manuals of prayer. It is enough simply to shout out of despair "Help!" and you will be heard.

Very often we do not find sufficient intensity in our prayer, sufficient conviction, sufficient faith, because our despair is not deep enough. We want God in addition to so many other things we have, we want his help, but simultaneously we are trying to get help wherever we can, and we keep God in store for our last push. We address ourselves to the princes and the sons of men, and we say "O God, give them strength to do it for me." Very seldom do we turn away from the princes and sons of men and say, "I will not ask anyone for help. I would rather have your help." If our despair comes from sufficient depth, if what we ask for, cry for, is so essential that it sums up all the needs of our life, then we find words of prayer and we will be able to reach the core of the prayer, the meeting with God.

— *Beginning to Pray*, 41

THE MOTHER OF GOD IN PRAYER

When we turn to the Mother of God in prayer, we should realize more often than we do that any prayer we offer to the
Mother of God means this: "Mother, I have killed your son.
If you forgive me, I can be forgiven." If you withhold forgiveness nothing can save me from damnation. And it is amazing
that the Mother of God, in all that is revealed in the Gospel,
has made us understand, and made us bold to come to her with
this very prayer, because there is nothing else we can say. To
us she is the Mother of God. She is the one who brought God
himself into our earthly situation. In that sense we insist on this
term "Mother of God." Through her God became man. He was
born into the human situation through her. And she is not to us
simply an instrument of the Incarnation. She is the one whose
personal surrender to God, her love of God, her readiness to be
whatever God wills, her humility in the sense in which I have
spoken about it to you already, is such that God could be born
of her. There is, in one of our great saints and theologians of the
fourteenth century, a passage on the Mother of God in which
he says, "The Incarnation would have been as impossible without the 'Here am I, the handmaid of God' of the Virgin, just as
it would have been impossible without the will of the Father."
Here there is a total co-operation between her and God. Speaking of the Incarnation and the attitude of the Blessed Virgin, I
think an English writer has put it in a remarkable way: Charles
Williams in his novel *All Hallows' Eve*. He says of the Incarnation that what makes its uniqueness is that "one day a virgin
of Israel was capable of pronouncing the sacred name with all
her heart, all her mind, all her being, all her body, in such a
way that in her word became flesh." I think this is a very good
theological statement that signifies the place that she has in the
Incarnation.

We love her, we feel that perhaps in her in a peculiar way
we see the Word of God spoken by Paul, who says, "My power
is made manifest in weakness." We can see this frail virgin of

Israel, this frail girl, defeating sin in her, defeating hell, defeating everything by the power of God that is in her. And this is why at moments like persecutions, when indeed the power of God is made manifest in nothing but weakness, the Blessed Virgin stands out so miraculously, so powerfully in our eyes. If she could defeat earth and hell, then we have in her a tower of strength and one who can intercede and save, and we mark the fact that in her there is no discrepancy with the will of God, that she is in perfect harmony with him, by using a formula of prayer that we use only for God and for her, "Save us." We don't say "Pray for us." *— Beginning to Pray,* 72

We must now say a few words about liturgical prayer. This prayer, which is always going on in the Church, may seem to lack spontaneity. It is indeed rigidly structured, because its aim is not only to express collective human spontaneity, but also to educate it. It is also an expression of beauty, but not just of the beauty that is present but of what the world could be, what God wishes it to be. We could discuss many details of the Liturgy of the Orthodox Church, the actions, the icons, the Bible readings. The Liturgy is a school for spirituality, it is a situation and an encounter with God and the world in God. It has its own spontaneity which goes beyond the actual spontaneity of each of its members. It is the holy spontaneity, of the community already fulfilled and in God. In the sacraments we come face to face with God not only through the word and its invisible grace but also through visible things. The waters of baptism become the primordial waters of life and also the water promised by Christ to the Samaritan woman. In the bread and wine, which have already become the body and blood of Christ, we prefigure the day when God will be all in all. In the Church we encounter God and the world in God. The Christian must also meet the world in all its sadness and serve it like the son of God made man. He must be totally involved in this Incarnation, it is part of being human and in it his prayer becomes intercession and intercession becomes the sacrifice of Calvary.

— Courage to Pray, 61

INTERCESSION

Christians spend their time interceding, and at times I listen to these intercessions with fear because to me intercession means an involvement that may spell death; and I am frightened when I hear a congregation of people interceding for one need after the other, piling up on their shoulders all the needs of the world just for the time Evensong lasts. After that they put it down on God's shoulders, and they go out elevated with a new emotion.

About ten years ago I came back from India. I was asked in London to speak at a rather big meeting about hunger. I spoke about what I had seen and what had wounded me very deeply with all the passion and violence I am capable of. For a while the people sat and listened, and then when we came out I stood at the west door shaking hands, and a lady came up to me and said, "Thank you for the entertaining evening." That is intercession very often with us. We have spied a need, we have become aware of a tragedy, and then from the security of our living, we turn to God, and say, "O Lord, haven't you noticed that? What are you doing about it? And this? And that? Aren't you forgetful of your duties to mankind?" This is not intercession. "Intercession" comes from a Latin word that means to take a step that brings you to the center of a conflict, and in the image of Christ, in the person of Christ, we see that intercession means taking a step that is definitive — once and for all he becomes man, not for a while.   — God and Man, 43

PRAYER ANSWERED AND UNANSWERED

The following short selection is another example of extremely practical prayer. When during the 1950s Metropolitan Anthony lived with his mother and grandmother at a house owned by the Church (known as Parish House), the property became infested with mice. One of his pious lady parishioners suggested he might use the prayer of St. Basil for the expulsion of various animals and pests, beginning with bears and wolves and finishing with insects, and including all kinds of creatures in between. He related many times how he — or rather St. Basil — rid the house of the mice and used the abbreviated story in this selection as an example of the effectiveness of prayer to the saints. In answer to the question, "Is liturgical prayer a means to communion with the saints?" Metropolitan Anthony replied:

It can be, of course. At times all we can do is to offer a prayer and say to the saint, "I don't really believe that this can work, but you who spoke these words, pray with me and on your faith let this prayer mount towards God." I had this experience once when I read the prayer called "intercession" by St. Basil the Great. I said to him, "I don't really believe that this can work, but you did, you prayed this prayer. Pray with me and all I can do is offer it together with you, on your faith. I prayed the prayer, and received answer to it.

He claimed that he waited for a mouse to appear, read the prayer to him, and then said, "Go and tell your friends, and don't come back again." And from that day, all the mice disappeared from the house.   — *Practical Prayer, 3*

MIRACLES

A miracle is not the breaking of the laws of the fallen world; it is the reestablishment of the Kingdom of God; a miracle happens only if we believe that the law depends not on the power but on the love of God. Although we know that God is almighty, as long as we think that he does not care, no miracle is possible; to work it God would have to enforce his will, and that he does not do, because at the very core of his relationship to the world, even fallen, there is his absolute respect for human freedom and rights. The moment you say: "I believe, and that is why I turned to you," implies: "I believe that you will be willing, that there is love in you, that you are actually concerned about every single situation." The moment that grain of faith is there the right relationship is established and a miracle becomes possible.

Apart from this type of "if," which refers to our doubt in the love of God and which is wrong, there is a legitimate category of "if." We can say: "I am asking this, if it is according to thy will, or if it is for the best, of if there is no secret evil intention in me when I ask," and so on. All these "ifs" are more than legitimate, because they imply a diffident attitude to our own selves; and every prayer of petition should be an "if-prayer."

— Living Prayer, 71

PRAYER FOR THE DEAD

What does it mean to pray for the dead? Are we asking the Lord to act unjustly? Certainly not. By our prayer, we bear witness that the dead have not lived in vain. We show that as well as the many worthless things they did in their lives, they also sowed the seed of charity. We pray for them with love and gratitude; we remember their presence among us. And our prayer for them must be supported by our lives. If we do not bear fruit in our lives of what the dead have taught us, our prayer for them will be feeble indeed. We must be able to say, "Lord, Lord, this man lived and made me love him, he gave me examples to follow and I follow them." The day will come when we shall be able to say, "The good that you see in my life is not mine; he gave me it, take it and let it be this for his glory, perhaps for his forgiveness...."

The life of each one of us does not end at death on this earth and birth into heaven. We place a seal on everyone we meet. This responsibility continues after death, and the living are related to the dead for whom they pray. In the dead we no longer belong completely to the world; in us the dead still belong to history. Prayer for the dead is vital; it expresses the totality of our common life.   *— Courage to Pray, 59*

Several years ago an old man in his middle eighties came to see me. He wanted advice because he could not continue to live in the agony that had been his for some sixty years. In the course of the civil war in Russia he had killed a girl whom he loved and who loved him. They loved one another dearly. They intended to be married, but in the course of the shooting she had suddenly run across his line of fire and it was too late to deflect his shot.

For sixty years he could not find peace. Not only had he cut down a life that was infinitely precious to him, but he had cut short a life that was blossoming and that was infinitely precious to the girl he loved. He told me that he had prayed, begged forgiveness of the Lord, gone to confession, made penance, received absolution and communion — done everything that his imagination and the imagination of those to whom he turned suggested, but he could never find peace.

In the inspiration of an intense, searing sympathy and compassion, I said to him: "You can turn to Christ whom you have not murdered, to priests whom you have not harmed. Why haven't you ever thought of turning to the girl that you killed?"

He was surprised. Cannot God forgive? Is he not the only one who can forgive the sins of men on earth? And indeed, of course, it is so. But I suggested to him that if the girl whom he had shot could forgive, could intercede for him, even God could not pass her by.

There is a story about the prophet Daniel in which Daniel prays, and God says to him that his prayer is in vain. This is because an old woman who has a grudge against him is praying against Daniel's prayer, and her prayer is like a strong wind that blows down like smoke the prayer that he hoped would ascend to heaven.

That was the image, perhaps, that came to me subconsciously. I suggested to him that he should sit down after evening prayers and tell this girl about these sixty years of mental agony, of a heart laid to waste, of the pain he had endured, ask her forgiveness and then ask her also to intercede for him and to ask the Lord to send peace into his heart if she had forgiven. And he did it, and peace came. So what is left undone on earth can be fulfilled. What has been a failure on earth can later be healed — but years of pain and remorse, of tears and loneliness, may be the price.

— *Living Orthodoxy in the Modern World*, 87

UNANSWERED PRAYER

Before I enter into the subject of "Unanswered Prayer," I would like to pray to God that he might enlighten both me and you, because it is a difficult subject, yet such a vital one. It is one of the great temptations that everyone may meet on his way, which makes it very hard for beginners, and even for proficient people, to pray to God. Many times people pray, and it seems to them that they are addressing an empty heaven; quite often it is because their prayer is meaningless, childish.

I remember the case of an old man telling me that when he was a child he prayed for several months that he would be given by God the amazing gift that his uncle possessed — that of every evening taking his teeth out of his mouth, and putting them into a glass of water — and he was terribly happy later on that God did not grant his wish. Often our prayers are as puerile as this, and of course they are not granted. Quite frequently when we pray we believe that we are praying rightly, but we pray for something that involves other people, of whom we do not think at all. If we pray for wind in our sails, we do not realize that it may mean a storm at sea for others, and God will not grant a request that affects others badly.

Besides those two obvious points, there is another side to unanswered prayer that is more basic and deep: there are cases when we pray to God from all our heart for something that, from every angle, seems to be worthy of being heard, and yet there is nothing but silence, and silence is much harder to bear than refusal. If God said "No," it would be a positive reaction of God's, but silence is, as it were, the absence of God and that leads us to two temptations: when our prayer is not answered, we either doubt God, or else we doubt ourselves. What we doubt in God is not his might, his power to do what we wish, but we doubt his love, his concern. We beg for something essential and he does not even seem to be concerned; where is his love and his compassion? This is the first temptation.

There is another: we know that if we had as much faith as a mustard seed, we could move mountains and when we see that nothing budges, we think, "Does that mean that the faith I have got is adulterated, false?" This again is untrue, and there is another answer: if you read the Gospel attentively, you will see that there is only one prayer in it that was not answered. It is the prayer of Christ in the Garden of Gethsemane, and yet we know that if once in history God was concerned for the one who prayed, it was then for his son, before his death, and also we know that if ever perfect faith was exemplified, it was in his case, but God found that the faith of the divine sufferer was great enough to bear silence.

God withholds an answer to our prayers not only when they are unworthy but when he finds in us such greatness, such depth — depth and power of faith — that he can rely upon us to remain faithful even in the face of his silence.

I remember a young woman with an incurable disease. After years of the awareness of God's presence, she suddenly sensed God's absence — some sort of real absence — and she wrote to me saying, "Pray to God, please, that I should never yield to the temptation of building up an illusion of his presence, rather than accept his absence." Her faith was great. She was able to stand this temptation and God gave her this experience of his silent absence.

Remember these examples, think them over because one day you will surely have to face the same situation.

— Living Prayer, 120

Metropolitan Anthony summed up his talks to unbelievers, on which his book "Beginning to Pray" was based, with the following words, which encapsulate all his thoughts and indeed his own experience, of prayer.

In the process of searching you will have endured pain, anguish, hope, expectation — all the range of human emotions. God will have been the desired one, and he will have been the frustrating one. He will have been the one you long for and the one you hate because he escapes you, the one you love beyond everything, without whom you cannot live, and whom you cannot forgive, because he does not respond, and many other things. And out of this search there will gradually emerge words that you can speak to God out of your own experience of the quest of the Grail, words that are your own. You may discover that they coincide with many words that others have used. Then they will cease to be anonymous words; they will be words that you have in common with other people but that have become truly yours. But do not use words that are in the common dictionary, words that do not belong to you. When you begin to hear a chain rattling on the door, when you have a feeling that it will open, then come out with the words that are your own and call God by the name that he has won in your own life. At that moment you will have met. In the ever deepening and enriching relationship that follows, you will have a great deal of time to discover other words, to discard the words of hatred and anguish. Like the martyrs spoken of in the Book of Revelation, you will say at a certain moment, "Thou hast been right in all Thy ways." And these words then will wipe out all the words of bitterness, all the names that sound cruel; but you will keep names that are personal, that are your own, and that will be a real relationship and a real way of being related to the living God.   — *Beginning to Pray,* 69

4

Orthodox Spirituality

As Metropolitan Anthony explains below, anyone seeking to embark seriously on the spiritual life should do so under the guidance of a spiritual father. He held his own spiritual father, Father Afanasy, in very great reverence.

I would like to define the meaning of the word "spirituality." Usually when we speak of spirituality we are talking of clear expressions of our spiritual life, such as prayer and asceticism as in such books as those of Theophan the Recluse. It seems to me, however, that spirituality consists of whatever is inspired in us by the Holy Spirit. Spirituality is not as we usually define it, but is the expression of the mysterious effect of the Holy Spirit.

This immediately puts us in a very particular position regarding spirituality, because we are not talking of educating a person according to certain principles and teaching him to develop in prayer or asceticism according to certain stereotyped conventions. Spirituality, in our terms, consists of the fact that the confessor or spiritual father, at whatever stage he finds himself, should be vigilant regarding the work of the Holy Spirit in a person: that he will inspire his actions, that he will protect him against temptations and falling away, against hesitation through lack of faith, so that spiritual activity might appear both much less active and much more significant than we often think.

Before going further, I want to say something about the role of the spiritual father. It is not a concept with a single meaning. I think there are two kinds of confessors.

On the most basic level a confessor is a priest who has been given the grace of priesthood and who carries within himself not only the right but the strength to perform the Mysteries — the Eucharist, Baptism, anointing with oil, but also the mystery of Confession, that is, the reconciliation of man with God. The great danger to which a young, inexperienced priest, full of enthusiasm and hope, is subject consists in the fact that sometimes young people leaving theological college imagine that being ordained has also bestowed on them wisdom and experience, and "the ability to discern spirits." They become what in the ascetic literature are called "young elders," that is, while not having yet achieved spiritual maturity, not yet having even that knowledge which gives people personal experience, they think that they have been taught everything that can help them take a repentant sinner by the hand and lead him from earth to heaven.

Unfortunately, this happens all too often and in all countries: a young priest, through the strength of his spirituality, not because he is spiritually experienced and not because God has brought him to this, begins to direct his spiritual children with "orders" — do not do this, but do that, do not read this literature, go to church, bow down to the ground. And as a result we get a caricature of spiritual life in his victims, who do everything they are told, doing what the ascetics did — but the latter acted like this on account of their own spiritual experience and not because they were trained animals. And for such a spiritual father it is a catastrophe, because he encroaches on a territory where he has neither the right nor the experience to encroach. I insist on this because this is a daily problem for the priesthood.

An elder can only become an elder through the blessing of God. It is a charismatic event, a gift. One cannot learn to be an elder, just as one cannot choose one's own path into genius. We can all wish to be geniuses, but we understand full well that Beethoven or Mozart, Leonardo da Vinci or Rublev were given their genius, which one cannot learn in any school, which one cannot even learn through long experience, but which is a God-given gift of grace.

I insist on this maybe at too great length because it seems to me that this is a vital theme — maybe in Russia more than in the West, because the priest's role in Russia is much more central. Often young priests — young either in age or in their spiritual maturity — "direct" their spiritual children instead of teaching them how to attain maturity.

To teach people how to mature is to tend them as a gardener tends his flowers and his plants: one has to know the nature of the soil, one has to know the nature of the plant, one has to know the circumstances in which they are placed, both climatic and otherwise, and only then can one be of help. And that is all that one can do — to help the plant to develop in a way that is natural to it through its own being. One Western spiritual writer said that a spiritual child can only be brought towards himself, and the road into that life is at times a very long one. In the lives of the saints one can see that eminent elders were able to achieve this, just as they could be themselves, but one has to bring to maturity in another person his unique, unrepeatable personality, and to give that person, and another, and a third, the ability to be themselves and not replicas of a given elder, or, even worse, stereotyped caricatures of him. . . .

Being an elder, as I have said, is a gift of grace. It is a state of spiritual genius, and so none of us can think of behaving as if we were elders. But there is another intermediary sphere, and that is spiritual fatherhood. And again, too often a young — or even a not-so-young — priest, simply because he is called "Father So-and-so," imagines that he is not simply a confessor, but indeed a spiritual father, in the sense in which St. Paul said "You have many mentors, but I have brought you in Christ," and the same was said in his time by St. Seraphim of Sarov. Spiritual fatherhood consists in the fact that some man — and he may not even be a priest — has brought another to the spiritual life, someone who, having looked at him, as the old saying goes, saw in his eyes and on his face the light of eternal life, and because of this could come up to him and ask him to be his teacher and his guide.

A father is of one blood with his son and, in the spiritual life, a spiritual father is of one spirit with his pupil and can guide him, because there is between them a true harmony not only of the spirit, but of the soul. You probably remember how, in its time, the Egyptian desert was full of ascetics and spiritual teachers. However, people did not choose a spiritual guide for themselves because of his outstanding fame, did not go to the person of whom most good was spoken, but found for themselves a spiritual guide whom they understood and who understood them.

This is very important, because spiritual obedience does not lie in blindly doing what someone says, someone who has physical, material, or spiritual power of the soul over you. Obedience lies in the fact that the pupil, having found a guide for himself, in whom he believes implicitly, and in whom he sees what he is himself searching for, takes heed not only of his every word, but listens to his tone of voice and tries to implant in himself the personality of his mentor with all his spiritual experience, to enter into communion with that experience and to outgrow it, becoming a person who has outgrown the stature he could attain through his own efforts. Obedience is first of all striving to listen and to hear not only with one's mind, not only with one's ears, but with one's whole being, with an open heart, with reverential contemplation, the spiritual mystery of another person.

Your spiritual father who bore you, or took you in after your spiritual birth, must act as a father to you. He must have a deep reverence for the way in which the Holy Spirit works in you. The spiritual father, in fact like any conscientious parish priest, must be in a position (and this sometimes requires effort, meditation, and a reverential attitude to the pupil) to see in the man that beauty of God's image which is never taken away, even if that man is damaged by sin. The spiritual father must see in him an icon, which has suffered from life's circumstances, or from human carelessness, or from blasphemy; he must see in him an icon and venerate what remains in him of that icon, and because of the divine beauty that is in him, must work towards eliminating from him everything that disfigures that image of God. Father Evgraf Kovalevsky, when he was still a layman, once said to me: "When God looks at a person, he does not see either virtue, which may not exist, or success, which may not have been achieved, but he sees the unshakeable, shining beauty of his own image." And so, if a spiritual father is not able to see in a person this eternal beauty, or to see in him the beginnings of a vocation to become a god-man in Christ's image, then he cannot guide him, because a man is not built up, he is not constructed, but he is helped to grow to the measure of his own calling. — *Encounter,* 262

THE HOLY SPIRIT

The "young man" of whom Metropolitan Anthony speaks here is in fact himself. He described this incident many times relating it in the first person.

I remember a young man speaking to me once ages back, who had become a Christian and was asking himself, "What does it mean that the Holy Spirit can come, and what does he do when he does?" And he told me that he was on a bus reflecting on that and asking, well, God more than himself. And suddenly when the bus swerved he had an awareness that something had rushed into him, and from that moment he began to *love* in a way he had never been able to love before. It was the rush *into* him of another presence. I think it does happen. If we have nothing to say to the Spirit, but "Come" and when he has come "Thank you that you are there," and then listen to him teaching us, in ineffable groanings, to pray gropingly while we are incapable of doing better, then at moments we will be able to say "Father" to one before whom otherwise we would simply prostrate ourselves in awesome adoration. At other moments we can be quiet and perceive his presence as one can listen and perceive the freshness of a running brook. An experience within us does not mean that we are so identified with it that we cannot discern that there are two things.   *— Our Life in God,* 15

When we speak of the Holy Spirit or when we say that God is spirit, what we do is to deny something within our concrete experience, and not describe something that is beyond our direct experience. When we say that God is spirit, we say simply that he is not matter as we know it, that he is something quite different. In that sense it is a negative description that belongs already without the word, to that form of theology which is negative theology, apophatic theology, a theology of paradoxes, a theology that uses words to point towards the ineffable — that which can be neither described nor put into words and yet which must be indicated somehow in speech.

One could avoid speech. In Siberia there were pagan tribes that had deliberately rejected every human word for God. And when in conversation they wanted to indicate God they raised their hand towards heaven. This is possible in a civilization of direct communication by speech. It is no longer possible in a civilization of books. But whatever words we use we have got to be aware of the fact that we are not describing, we are not defining what God is, because the very thing we know about God is that he is beyond defining, beyond describing. So that when we say of God that he is Spirit, when we speak of the Holy Spirit in particular, we do not mean to give a concrete definition or any description of what he is. We point towards the fact that he is beyond our conceptual knowledge, beyond every formulation, that he is what we don't know, and this is what we mean to say by saying that he is spirit as contrasted with us.

Of course, there are a great many ways in which the word "spirit" is used in Scripture: the spirit of man, the spirits in the plural, meaning the angels and the demons. Also there is the way in which we use the word "spirit," when we say the spirit of a nation, the spirit of a group of people, which means in the end something indefinable, intangible, but clearly recognizable as being specific, as being unique. And this is perhaps the direction in which we should think when we say that God is Spirit or when we speak of the Holy Spirit.

Now there is another approach, also scriptural, which brings us perhaps — if you do not forget my first remarks — to a nearer understanding. You all remember the conversation that the Lord Jesus Christ had with Nicodemus one night and that is described in the book of St. John. You can picture the scene. The evening has come. Christ and Nicodemus are in the gathering darkness and in the cool of the night, standing or seated on the flat roof of one of the houses in Jerusalem. They speak of God and Nicodemus tries to understand. And Christ says: "God is spirit," and he goes on to say: "The Spirit bloweth where it listeth, and you do not know where it comes from and whither it goes," Now the word that Christ used, which is the Hebrew word *ruah,* corresponds exactly to the Greek and Latin words *pneuma* and *spiritus,* and all three in their basic meaning signify the breathing of the wind, the blowing of the wind.

Obviously Christ is not saying that God is like the wind in all respects. Materially the wind is made of things material, the air. What he says is, first of all, that like the wind God cannot be defined in shape and in substance. He escapes our grasp. The wind blows and you cannot retain it in your hands. The wind blows and you cannot give a shape to this blowing, not like a river that runs in a bed. On the other hand the wind is perceived, and it is perceived as a direct experience. What is characteristic of the wind is that we know it, not because we can observe it from outside, but because we perceive it as a personal experience. If you go back to the short description I gave you in the beginning, of Nicodemus and Christ standing on the flat top of a roof in the evening breeze, what it really conveys is this: the wind is blowing and you know it because your skin is refreshed, because you breathe more freely, because you can see your clothes moving softly in this blowing wind. You know for sure that the wind is blowing. Yet you have no idea where it comes from, where it will end its course. All you know about the blowing of the wind is that you are within it, that you are touched by it; you have a certainty about it because it is a personal, direct, experiential certainty.

This is an extremely important thing, because when you read what we have in the Scriptures concerning the Holy Spirit there are two claims concerning him. On the one hand, the Holy Spirit is known by mankind through experience and not otherwise. Christ is known as an event of history. He stands face to face with us. He is a "non-me," exactly in the same terms in which each of us with regard to each other is "not him," "not her." Christ therefore — not in all ways, but in a way — is external to us. Our knowledge of him is knowledge comparable to the knowledge we can possess of any other event in history, of a person in history, of events developing around a person. We can dissociate ourselves from him. We can accept him as our God or deny him, accept him as our Savior or reject him. We can believe his word or disbelieve his word. We may love him or dislike him. We are free to relate to him as to an object outside us.

Not so with the Holy Spirit, because the Holy Spirit is perceived by us *only* within our experience, the way in which the wind that was blowing around Nicodemus was a certainty of his experience, not a certainty of objective knowledge. I know that you could argue with me that one has discovered a great deal about the wind and so on, but this is not what the Scriptures convey.

So our only knowledge of the Holy Spirit is experience. And this is perhaps the reason why in St. Mark's Gospel we are told that every blasphemy against Christ can be forgiven, while a blasphemy spoken against the Holy Spirit cannot. Christ can be misinterpreted. We may not recognize him. We may make an error of judgment. We may not be mature enough to accept him, because he is outside of us and we must relate to him from within towards him and from within him towards us. But we cannot deny any of the experiences connected with the Holy Spirit, because they are our own experience.

To give you an image: someone standing in the freezing cold in the street may look through a window and see in a grate

the flames of an open fire. If it is his first experience of seeing and experiencing fire and he is told that fire is something
that warms you to the core, he would shrug his shoulders and
say: "No, it doesn't. The flames are dancing over there but I
am totally frozen." On the contrary, if you find yourself in a
room where... if you see a fire in the grate, you are warmed,
and still deny that the fire has brought warmth to you, there
is no way of making you free from the error, because you are
denying not an objective fact outside of you, but a real fact
within you. You are either insane or a liar, but there is no other
way of assessing your condition. The first, therefore, may be an
error of judgment, a sign of ignorance, an inability to relate to
an objective, external fact. The second is a denial of what you
know to be true and which you reject. So what we know of the
Holy Spirit — and this you find throughout the Scriptures — is
something within you. For instance, the Spirit that lives in man
plumbs the depths of man. The Holy Spirit speaks within us
in "groanings ineffable" (Rom. 8:26). The Holy Spirit teaches
us to say, "Abba, Father" (Gal. 4:6; Rom. 8:15). The Holy
Spirit — and this is a Moffat translation — "moulds within us,
fashions within us the knowledge of God."

Well, all these things are within us. None of them is outside
of us. Obviously here the imagery breaks down because we may
well say that the wind touched Nicodemus on his skin and not
in his soul. But I am speaking of experience and no longer of the
wind at this moment. So all the knowledge we have of the Holy
Spirit personally, collectively, is experiential or none. "None"
does not exist, in a way: we all have some sort of touch of
God. But it is experiential. What we know of the Holy Spirit
as a Person is given us to know by God but not otherwise. And
this is the difficulty that theology has found throughout time in
speaking of the Holy Spirit. What we can say we can say from
within us, but it is so little, and it refers to his action. We will
come to that in a moment. What we can say about him as a Person is something that we cannot know and do not know and is
only a matter of revelation. And this is why Eastern theology
has always been sharply, determinedly opposed to any attempt

at working out logically the nature of the Holy Spirit within the Holy Trinity and has accepted simply by an act of faith the Living God and rejected the god of the philosophers of whom St. Paul speaks.

What we know about the Holy Spirit from the Scriptures you can find in short at the end of the fifteenth chapter of St. John's Gospel, the penultimate verse: "When the Comforter is come whom I will send unto you from the Father, even the Spirit of Truth Which proceedeth from the Father, he shall testify of me." What we know is that the Holy Spirit in the words of Christ himself proceeds from the Father, that he is sent to his disciples by the Son, and that teaching us he acts upon us. We know him within us as a divine energy that makes us into new creatures. We know about him from Christ himself.

You know that one speaks of the "generation" of the Son and the "procession" of the Holy Spirit. Here again I would say that it is infinitely important not to imagine that these words describe actual events. First of all, they do not describe events in time, because there was no *moment* when the Father was alone, when he subsequently gave birth to his Son, nor was the origin of the Holy Spirit subsequently or simultaneously proceeding from him. When we speak of God we speak of a timelessness totally beyond any kind of understanding on our part. What the words signify is that the Spirit and the Son relate to the Father in two different ways — and the word "generation" has been used naturally because in speaking of Father and Son the word "generation" comes quite naturally, the one being born of the other. The expression "proceeds" means really, if you look at what was written by the Fathers, that the Spirit has his origin in the Father, that as it were he flows from him, but he is not an emanation in the sense in which oriental religion thinks of emanations.   — *Our Life in God, 2*

Remember what is written of the work of the Spirit: "But the fruit of the Spirit is love, joy, peace, long-suffering ... against such there is no law" (Gal. 5:22–23). This shows to us in the right order what is the effect of the Holy Spirit's coming to us, that there settle within us quiet, order, joy, and lucidity in the heart, the quelling of passions, the mind's irradiation, a fervor for God, sobriety, and a mortification of the flesh. We know all this through experience, because each one of us at some moment experiences this. Only we forget; and we forget because we are inattentive: we are at one and the same time making much of ourselves and inattentive to ourselves.

On Mount Tabor, at the Transfiguration of the Lord, the Lord did not change. The Lord was the same from the very beginning. He was the incarnate Son of God, nothing happened to him at that moment, but something happened to his disciples. He shone out in front of them and they saw his glory insofar as they were able. And then they ceased to see, because this vision of glory plunged them into horror and they fell down flat, and Peter began to say some mad words: let us put up three tabernacles — it is good for us here. He did not know how to express what was going on in his soul. 　　　　 — *Encounter,* 123

All true prayer, that is prayer made in humility and surrender to God, is sooner or later quickened by the grace of the Holy Spirit. This grace becomes the force behind every action and thus everything in life. It ceases to be an activity and becomes our very being, the presence in us of him, who fills all things and leads them to their own fullness. 　　 — *Courage to Pray,* 62

ASCETICISM

The extent to which asceticism is seen as part of the ordinary Christian life in Orthodoxy is perhaps surprising to Christians from the Western Churches. Fasting, the practice of the Jesus Prayer, as well as the long Church services based on monastic services, are all part of a committed Orthodox Christian's life.

Metropolitan Anthony's first ambition, as a young man, was to lead the ascetic monastic life. He was never able to do this, as the following selections show; even after becoming a monk he always remained "in the market place," as he put it.

Nevertheless, asceticism remained central to his understanding of Christianity.

When I had finished secondary school, I wondered what I should do. I thought of becoming a Desert Father; but it turned out that there were very few deserts left, and that with my passport I would not be allowed to go to any desert, and besides I had a mother and grandmother, who had to be supported in some way, and this would be inconvenient from a desert! Then I wanted to become a priest, and later decided to enter a monastery on Valaam, and in the end all this came together in one idea. I do not know how this idea came about, probably from a combination of various ideas: that I could take monastic vows secretly, become a doctor, move to somewhere in France where there were Russians who were too poor and too few to have a Church and a priest, and so become their priest.

...I prayed, I fasted, and with this in view [the decision to become a monk] I made all possible mistakes.

I fasted to exhaustion, I prayed till I drove everybody mad at home, and so on. It usually happens that when somebody in the house wants to clamber up into heaven, the other inhabitants become saints because everyone has to have patience with him, to resign themselves to the situation, and to bear everything that the zealot does.   — *Encounter*, 202

One of the characteristics of a genuinely healthy spiritual life is temperance. We know in ordinary speech what sobriety means in comparison to drunkenness. One can get drunk in various ways, and not only through wine. Everything that fascinates us so much that we no longer can remember God or ourselves, nor the basic values of life: this is a form of drunkenness. It has no connection to what I have called inspiration — the inspiration of a scholar, of an artist, to whom God has given the ability to see behind the outward form to that which surrounds it: a certain depth of being, which he can draw out and express in sounds, or lines, or colors so as to make it accessible to the people

around it who were blind to it. But when we forget specifically that very meaning revealed by them and create an object
of delight out of that which should be the object of contemplation — then we lose our sobriety. In Church life it happens so
often and so destructively, when people come to church because
of the singing, or because of those emotions that are aroused
by the harmony of the mystery of the divine service, when God
is no longer in the center of everything but only the experience
that is the fruit of his presence. The essential feature of Orthodox piety, of Orthodox spirituality, is sobriety, which transfers
everything of value and its entire meaning from itself to God.
                                                    — *Encounter,* 228

I do not speak now of the forms of asceticism or the way in
which one does it, but we must learn to be free, and to be free,
we must acquire mastery over ourselves. This is terribly important, and to achieve that, we must learn to look and learn, but
not only to look at people and situations — look at God, and
learn and hear. Obedience is vital. To obey the will of God
requires training. The will of God is madness, the will of God
is paradoxical. You cannot adhere to the will of God for good
reasons. More often what he often asks is an act of folly that
we would not otherwise dare to commit. Remember Abraham:
God promised him a son, and the son was born. He promised
that the son would be a beginning of a generation of people
more numerous than the sands of the shores, and Abraham
believed him. And then God commanded him to take his son
and to bring him, a blood offering, to him, and Abraham did it.
He did not tell him, "That contradicts your previous injunction;
this is contrary to your promise." he trusted the Lord and did
what the Lord said at that moment, leaving the Lord to fulfill
his promises the way he knows.

This happens to us also. We are called to act day after day,
moment after moment, according to the will of God revealed
within that moment when the difference between Christian
action and just action resides in the fact that action must be
planned, action must not contradict action. There are no returns

and moves back and sideways; it must be a straight course. If we want to act within the will of God, we must be like Christ, who listens and proclaims the word, who gazes attentively at God who is at work, and when he has seen performs the action that is implied in the willing, in the thinking, in the rich creative imaginings of God. This we must learn, but to do this, we must learn to master ourselves and become capable of acting not only when we agree, not only when we understand, but when we disagree somewhere within the old Adam in us, or when we cannot understand but say, "I trust you, I will act with folly."

— *God and Man,* 122

THE JESUS PRAYER

One of the best-known aspects of Orthodox asceticism is the practice of the Jesus Prayer: the repetition of the words, "Lord Jesus Christ, Son of God, have mercy on me, a sinner." Metropolitan Anthony was well aware of the pitfalls that could be encountered by overenthusiastic people and always advised caution. He wrote of it in various places, including an important introduction to the English version of the Russian classic The Way of a Pilgrim.

A last way in which we can pray is the use, more or less continuous, of a vocal prayer that serves as a background, a walking stick, throughout the day and throughout life. What I have in mind now is something specifically used by the Orthodox. It is what we call the "Jesus prayer," a prayer centered on the name of Jesus: "Lord Jesus Christ, son of God, have mercy on me, a sinner." This prayer is used by monks and nuns, but it is also used by our lay people. It is the prayer of stability, because it is the prayer that is not discursive — we do not move from one thought to the other. It is a prayer that places us face to face with God through a profession of faith concerning him, and it defines a situation concerning us. It is the profession of faith that, according to the mind of most Orthodox ascetics and mystics, is a summing up of the whole Gospels.

— Beginning to Pray, 31

All the messages of the Gospel, and more than the messages, the reality of the Gospel, is contained in the name, in the person of Jesus. If you take the first half of the prayer you will see how it expresses our faith in the Lord: "Lord Jesus Christ, Son of God." At the heart we find the name of Jesus; it is the name before whom every knee shall bow (Isa. 45:23), and when we pronounce it we affirm the historical event of the Incarnation. We affirm that God, the Word of God, co-eternal with the father, became man, and that the fullness of the godhead dwelt in our midst (Col. 2:9) bodily in his person.

To see in the man of Galilee, in the prophet of truth, the incarnate Word of God, God become man, we must be guided by the Spirit, because it is the Spirit of God who reveals to us both the Incarnation and the lordship of Christ. We call him Christ, and we affirm thereby that in him were fulfilled the prophecies of the Old Testament. To affirm that Jesus is the Christ implies that the whole history of the Old Testament is ours, that we accept it as the truth of God. We call him Son of God, because we know that the Messiah expected by the Jews, the man who was called "son of David" by Bartimaeus, is the incarnate Son of God. These words sum up all we know, all we believe about Jesus Christ, from the Old Testament to the New, and from the experience of the Church through the ages. In these few words we make a complete and perfect profession of faith.

But it is not enough to make this profession of faith; it is not enough to believe. The devils also believe and tremble (James 2:19). Faith is not sufficient to work salvation. It must lead to the right relationship with God; and so, having professed, in its integrity, sharply and clearly, our faith in the lordship and in the person, in the historicity and in the divinity of Christ, we put ourselves face to face with him, in the right state of mind: "Have mercy on me, a sinner."

These words "have mercy" are used in all the Christian Churches and, in Orthodoxy, they are the response of the people to all the petitions suggested by the priest. Our modern translation "have mercy" is a limited and insufficient one. The Greek word that we find in the Gospel and in the early liturgies is *eleison*. *Eleison* is of the same root as *elaion*, which means olive tree and the oil from it.

... The oil speaks first of all of the end of the wrath of God, of the peace that God offers to the people who have offended him; further it speaks of God healing us in order that we should be able to live and become what we were called to be; and as he knows that we are not capable with our own strength of fulfilling either his will or the laws of our own created nature, he pours his grace abundantly on us (Rom. 5:20). He gives us power to do what we could not otherwise do.

... If we turn back to the words of the Jesus Prayer, "Lord Jesus Christ, Son of God, have mercy on me, a sinner," we see that the first words express with exactness and integrity the Gospel faith in Christ, the historical Incarnation of the Word of God, and the end of the prayer expresses all the complex rich relationships of love that exist between God and his creatures.

The Jesus Prayer is known to innumerable Orthodox, either as a rule of prayer or in addition to it, as a form of devotion, a short focal point that can be used at any moment, whatever the situation.

Numerous writers have mentioned the physical aspects of the prayer, the breathing exercises, the attention paid to the beating of the heart and a number of other minor features. The Philokalia is full of detailed instructions about the prayer of the heart, even with references to the Sufi technique. Ancient and modern Fathers have dealt with the subject, always coming to the same conclusion: never to attempt the physical exercises without strict guidance by a spiritual father.

— *Living Prayer*, 84

There are a certain number of preliminary conditions that must be satisfied by the man who wishes to engage in the Jesus

Prayer, with God's help and under the direction of his spiritual father. First, an awareness, clear or confused, of the horror into which is plunged the man who is "outside God," walled up in the deadly isolation of his ego. As Theophan the Recluse teaches: "A self-centered man is like a thin shaving of wood curling up around the void of his inner nothingness, cut off alike from the cosmos and the Creator of all things." Second, there must be the belief that life is found in God alone, and, third, there must be the will for conversion, that is to say, for the spiritual volte-face that makes us essentially and irrevocably strangers to a world sundered from God and sets us on a new plane of existence, that of God himself and the world in God.

Thus, as he embarks on his course, the Christian must make his peace with God, with his own conscience, with men and things; relinquish all care about himself, firmly purpose to forget himself, not to know himself, to kill in himself all greed, even for spiritual things, in order to know nothing but God alone.

Henceforward the worshiper must free himself from the bondage of the world by unconditional obedience — joyful, total, humble, and immediate; he must in all simplicity seek God, without hiding any of his wretchedness, without founding any hope on himself, in this active self-abandonment to God that is the spirit of watchfulness in humility, in veneration, with a sincere will to be converted, ready to die rather than give up the search.

There is no doubt that the most characteristic feature of the Jesus Prayer and of the hesychast (quietist) tradition in which it is grounded, the most precious legacy it has left to the Orthodox, is this indissoluble union of a physical and mental ascetic technique of minute exactness and extreme strictness in the demands it makes, with a high affirmation of the fundamental worthlessness of all technique and all artificial means in the mystery of the union of the soul with God — the mystery of mutual self-giving in love, in the fullness of liberty. Hence it is possible to use all ascetic methods, but with discernment, freedom, boldness: "All is lawful for me, but all is not expedient." This filial liberty and strict fidelity is the attitude of the Orthodox Church.   — *The Way of a Pilgrim*, ix

5

The Church

✝

THE NATURE OF THE CHURCH

The Church is a society of love. If those around us were to see in us people transformed by love, they would not ask which is the right God, and is there a God, and which religion is best. As the Apostle Paul said a long time ago, "For the Name of God is blasphemed among the Gentiles through you" (Rom. 2:14). The answer does not lie in good works but in love, because there are many kind people who are dry as sticks, in spite of doing everything that should be done — nobody will be drawn to God by this. But the God of love, the God who teaches us that the other is more important than oneself, that my neighbor is the person who needs me and not the one who happens to live near me — that is one of the criteria. In this sense, of course, we make many people question the Christian faith.   — *Encounter*, 107

What I want to say will probably offend a lot of people. I think that today the whole Christian world, including the world of Orthodoxy, has become cut off from the simplicity, the all-inclusiveness, and the triumphant beauty of the Gospels. Christ with his group of disciples founded a Church that was so deep, so all-embracing, so complete, that it contained within itself the whole universe. Over the centuries we have made the Church one of mankind's societies. We are smaller than the world in which we live, and when we speak of the conversion of this

world to Christianity, we are saying in fact that we should convert as many people as possible into being members of a limited
society. This, I consider, is our sin.

We should understand that the Christian Church, the believers, should be believers not only on account of their view of the
world but also in their lives, through their inner experience, and
that our part consists in bringing light into this world where it
is so dark and at times so frightening. The prophet Isaiah says:
"Comfort ye, comfort ye my people" (Isa. 40:1). Those were
God's words to him and, of course, also to us: "Comfort ye."
That means: understand in what sorrow the whole world exists,
both materially and in its confusion, and spiritually, through its
lack of God's grace. It means that we should bring comfort to
this world: God's tenderness, God's love, and God's concern,
which should enfold every person. There is no point in speaking
to a man about spiritual things when he is starving — feed him.
There is no point in saying that a man errs in his view of the
world when we fail to provide him with the living experience of
the Living God. And that is our position in the world today —
it is the position of people awaiting trial. The world, in turning away from God and from the Church, is saying to us: "You
Christians cannot give us anything that we need. You do not
give us God: you give us a view of the world. It is very doubtful
whether at its heart there is any living experience of God. You
do not give us instructions how to live — yours are as arbitrary
as those which we get from other people." We need to become
Christians — Christians in the manner of Christ and his disciples, and only then will the Church acquire not power — the
ability to coerce people — but authority — the ability to speak
such words that once any soul hears them it will shudder and
will open itself to the eternal depths.   — *Encounter,* 160

When we speak of the Church we are prone to define it in
terms that we take from our catechisms. All these descriptions
are true, and yet they are insufficient if we wish to comprehend
and know the Church. The reason for this is that the catechism,
which is now studied by children who are already Christians,

was originally intended for people who were not yet Christians; it was an introduction to the Church, and not a part of ecclesial life in its true depths. So what we find in it are definitions, explanations that are within reach of those who have not yet passed through the door leading into the Church, within reach of catechumens who are still outside the mysteries of the Liturgy, outside the prayer of the Church, which is conscious of itself and offers—with Christ, to Christ, and in the name of the living Christ—the articulated prayer of the created world. And thus these definitions, however true they may be, nevertheless leave us outside the Church.

. . . This is natural, because knowledge of the Church is above all an *experience* of the Church. Like everything that belongs to the divine realm, it is a knowledge made up of adoration, of communion, and of belonging. From this point of view, the Church appears to us as something very much deeper than a collection of definitions.

Yes, we are united by a single common faith, we possess the same sacraments, we serve the same Liturgy, we have a hierarchy that unites us all and holds us together in a visible and perceptible unity. But the profound nature of the Church, the profound experience of the Church, is defined differently.

Above all the Church is defined in the words of St. Paul: the Church is the Body of Christ (Rom. 7:4; 1 Cor. 10:16; 1 Cor. 12:27; Eph. 4:12). This is an expression that is either so familiar to us that it has lost its meaning, or, on the contrary, so strange that it no longer offers us anything at all. It is a combination of words whose meaning we must rediscover from generation to generation, especially because the word "body" has acquired over the centuries so many shades of meaning and has become, above all, a sociological reality: a trade association, an army corps, or a workers union. These are terms that define a society whose nature is only that of a group of people united to face a common task or in a common situation. But when we speak of the "Body of Christ," we speak of something much more real, much deeper than that; it is a term linked with the

Incarnation, and not with the cohesion of members who might afterwards separate.

In what sense, then, can it be said that we are the Body of Christ? In the realistic sense, I believe, as was brought out by a Russian theologian of the last century, the Church is an extension of the Incarnation. Each one of us is a *presence* of Christ, but in what sense are we an "incarnation"? In what sense is Christ really present in us? Can we take seriously such expressions as that of St. Paul: "...yet not I, but Christ liveth in me" (Gal. 2:20)? If this is so, what remains of us, if Christ lives in me and I no longer live? What reality has this? Has Christ simply taken the place of the human person?

First of all, this definition of the Church as Body, as organism, helps us at once to understand that it is not a whole made up out of parts that are separable one from the other. It is a whole that is not made up of parts, but of *members,* and of members that are eternally inseparable from the moment they unite in a body. This feeling of an unbreakable unity was very strong in antiquity, and was expressed in a remarkable way by Justin Martyr. Writing to one of his friends who had sinned gravely and was cut off from communion with the Church, he said: "Do you not realize that as long as you remain outside this living body, the body of Christ has a wound that no one can heal but you?" The Church then, is not a matter of members who are interchangeable; one cannot forget a presence simply because one no longer perceives it; one cannot replace someone who was there by someone who was not there. Someone who belongs to this Body belongs to it in a way that may even be tragic, but he belongs to it for ever....

The Church is revealed to us as something much more profound and much greater than any human society, whatever its character. The Church is revealed as the mystery of the meeting and the union between God, One in the Holy Trinity, and his creatures, whose dispersion, whose division is overcome and whose unity is realized anew, first in an act of faith and then in a mystery of communion. The Church is the presence of the Most

Holy Trinity in the midst of us and in us. It is the action of the life-giving Trinity in his creatures.

But the Church is not only glory. There is in the Church a poor and unhappy side; there is a glorious side and there is a tragic side. The poor and miserable side is ourselves; it is the empirical Church, the one that we see. It is not of her that we speak when we say: "I believe in One, Holy, Catholic and Apostolic Church." It is not in this empirical aspect by itself that we profess our faith, for that is what is visible — all too visible. In a certain sense we belong both to the world and, at the same time, already to the Church. As Father George Florovsky said, we are at once *in patria* and *in via;* we are already in the Church and we are on the way to enter it. So long as evil, sin, and death are not yet vanquished in us, we are still in the process of transformation. But nevertheless, in a deeper sense, we are already the children of God; we are the companions of God in his work of salvation. We are like the crew of a lifeboat: we know the will of God, we have been called to be the companions of his labors. He has told us that he no longer wants to call us servants, but friends; for the servant does not know what his master wants, while to us he has told all that he wants. And in this there is a mysterious glory, a radiance, a light.

And then there is a tragic side. Briefly, it is this: St. Paul says in his Epistle to the Colossians that we are like a colony of heaven on the earth; we are the representatives of a celestial metropolis in a strange land. And in spite of this, we still claim that we are citizens of this land; faced with kings and those who guide and possess the nations, we claim to be both totally integrated in earthly reality and to represent a reality that surpasses it. It is not surprising, therefore, that the world rejects us and that we appear to it as a sort of "fifth column," as traitors who pretend to be citizens of this world while recognizing the power of a king who is not of this world; as a group of people for whom the only law is the act of love, while they remain estranged from the law of the land. And this law of love is a danger and a threat to the land, because love implies renunciation of self even to the point of death. And also because to be in communion with Christ, to have with him a common life, means accepting the totality of his destiny, not only the glory that for us is yet to come, the eternal joy that for us is yet to come, but also his destiny in history: "I send you forth as lambs among wolves..." (Luke 10:3).

— The Living Body of Christ, 4

THE CHURCH AND THE EUCHARIST

How mysterious the Church is; one at the core, one at the root, and yet so painfully, monstrously divided.

In the communion service, in the Liturgy, after the words "The Holy Things to Them that are Holy" the priest breaks the Holy Bread, already consecrated, which is the Body of Christ and says "The Lamb of God is broken and distributed, which being ever broken, never is divided but halloweth them that partake thereof." Is that an image of the Church in history? If it is true that all those who believe in Christ, all those who through baptism have died with Christ and risen with him, if it is true that all those are at one with him, then it is true also that there is unity; but it is also so patently true that we are divided on all levels. Dare we say that we are so one with each other that nothing can break the bonds of solidarity and of love? Can we say that the Churches that call themselves Christ's own are so one that there is no divergence of faith, no competition, suspicion, mutual dislike, all things that are unthinkable in one body possessed of one spirit that is called to be to the world a revelation of the fact that God came into the world, into a world divided, a world broken, and, like the key of harmony in music, brought everything into oneness. Is it thinkable?

And yet so it is.

We may say that no one but the saints can experience that oneness of which we speak. But this is not enough. To say that only the saints experience it does not mean that we have a right to remain outsiders to it, and in our everyday life it is dividedness and separation that we perceive so painfully. Can we say that we love one another? Certainly not. We love a few, we ignore the many, we dislike or hate a number of people. Are we at one? Yes, at blessed moments, when prayer takes over, when God takes over and we forget ourselves and one another in a way, to see one another only in Christ; but otherwise, no.

. . . So let us be very, very careful. It is not greed that should bring us to communion; it is not the desire to receive something for ourselves, it is a desire to unite ourselves with Christ so as to be in conformity with him in thought, in heart, in mind, in action, in everything that is us, and ask him to make it possible by his power and grace. So again, again let us think of it. Is it possible that you have come simply in order to receive and not in order to share with Christ his own destiny? Can we say in the Lord's Prayer "forgive us as we forgive" if there is no forgiveness in us, and in that case how can we come to receive communion? Amen.   — Sermon on church and communion, Sunday, February 2, 1992

THE STRUCTURES OF THE CHURCH

The following originated as an address to the Diocesan Assembly of Metropolitan Anthony's own diocese. In answer to a question at the end: how much did he think his words would be understood in Russia today? He replied: very little. This piece was his personal understanding (although not unique to him) of what the Church should be; and he had tried to fashion his own diocese in this mold, hoping that it would be an example for others to follow — even, one day, in Russia itself. That has proved not to be the case. Metropolitan Anthony lived out much of what he says here. He lived simply, in a small flat at the rear of his cathedral, and acted as its caretaker.

There are two elements in the life of the Church. The one element by necessity is structured because we are imperfect, because we are on our way, because we must be guided, and, like a river that runs towards the sea, must have banks, since

otherwise we will become a bog. And on the other hand, there
is the living water that Christ gave to the Samaritan woman
that runs in this river.

There is in us already something fulfilled and something
imperfect. St. Ephraim the Syrian said that when God creates
a human being he puts at the core of his or her being the fullness of the Kingdom of God. If you prefer, one can say that he
puts there the perfect image of God. And the purpose of life is
to dig, deeper and deeper, until we reach this point and bring
it to the fore. So when we speak of structures in the Church,
we must remember that there is in the Church something that
cannot be structured, cannot be organized, cannot be limited by
rules and by laws. This is the action of the Holy Spirit within
each of us, and within the local body, or the body universal.
And this is very important because the Holy Spirit speaks to
us, each of us and all of us, either in inexpressible groanings or
with the clarity of the trumpet that calls us into battle.

But on the other hand, there is in us imperfection and frailty.
And therefore there must be structures that are like a scaffold-
ing, or like the banks of a river, or like a stick that one uses if
one is lame, to prevent us from collapsing.

Now the temptation for the Church, as for every other human
organization, is to structure itself according to worldly principles,
principles of hierarchy, of power — as a hierarchy of submission, a hierarchy of enslavement, of humiliation, of irrelevance.
Take the hierarchy of irrelevance, for instance. In more than one
community — practically speaking, very much in our Orthodox
communities, and theologically in Rome — the laity is an irrelevance. It is a flock to be guided. It has no right in and of itself
except to obey, to be directed towards the goal that, allegedly,
the hierarchy knows.

In its extreme form, the Church is conceived as a pyramid at
the top of which stands the Pope. To me, this is a heresy against
the nature of the Church, because no one but the Lord Jesus
Christ has a right to stand at the top of that pyramid. It is not
a question of whether this means that the Church will be well
administered, but of the very nature of the Church.

So if we eliminate the structures of power and the submission that goes with them, we must still ask ourselves what should be the structure of the Church. The structure that we are entitled to speak of is that which Christ defines when he says, "If anyone wants to be first, let him be a servant to all" (Mark 9:35). The hierarchy consists in service. The higher the servant allegedly is in rank, in titles, the lower he should be in terms of service. He should be the one who does the humblest service, and not the highest.

This is something that we must recapture. But it can be recaptured only if we recapture our understanding of the Church as a total body with a variety of functions and not a variety of bodies joined together one on top of the other. By this I mean that we must recapture the role, the dignity of the laity. The royal priesthood is forgotten. If it is not forgotten in manuals of theology, it is forgotten in the practice of life. And I would like to insist on that because I would like you to accept a point of view that is very important to me: dear to me and important to me.

By becoming a minister of the Church we do not stop being a member of the Body of Christ, of the *laos,* of the people of God. I was once introduced to a conference from which clergy were banned, but where I had to be admitted because I was a speaker, with the words: "Here is Metropolitan Anthony, who is a layman in clerical orders."

This is perfectly true. The laity, on one level, includes also the clergy, but with different functions. We must recapture this notion of the holiness and dignity of the laity. And unless we do this, we cannot think of structures that are an image of the Holy Trinity. We do not have in the Holy Trinity — I am about to say something quite blasphemous — a "top dog" with subservient slaves. God the Father is not the "boss" of the Trinity, with two "managers." It is true that the Fathers say that God creates the world with his two hands, the Son and the Holy Spirit. This is imagery applicable in that context. But basically there is a total equality of the three Persons of the Trinity. And there is also a total equality of all the members of the Church. There is no other way.

Of course, there is a hierarchical structure: a structure in which the one who is the best servant, who is the slave of others, is greatest in the eyes of God. But that is the point. This is made even less visible thanks to our liturgical practice, because our Eucharistic Liturgy has in its forms very much taken as a model the Byzantine imperial court. And so it is not difficult for a bishop to feel himself as the head of the body, surrounded by lesser and lesser ministers, and then a flock outside. But this is untrue.

The Liturgy is celebrated by the whole body, not by the ministers alone. And this is why I have said more than once that no one should come and receive communion who has not been present from the beginning of the service — unless, of course, a major impediment intervenes. Because otherwise he is not *making* the Liturgy. If someone arrives halfway through the Liturgy and claims to have communion, he is treating the Liturgy as though it were a restaurant in which various cooks are preparing the meal: he comes when he has the time and claims his portion.

This is very important: we must recover the notion that the laity *includes* the clergy. And in that case the different members of the ordained ministry will have their own proper place in the building of the Church.

. . . And so when we speak of the hierarchy we need to realize that we must recapture a true approach to hierarchy: a hierarchy of service, a hierarchy of humility, a hierarchy in which there is no dominion, no power. God chose to be powerless when he gave us freedom, the right to say "no" to whatever he says. But God in Christ, God in the Spirit has another quality. Not power, which is the ability to coerce, but authority, which is the ability to convince. And that is a very different thing.

Authority is that quality which a human being — and God — possesses of being able to convince, not force us to do something. And if our hierarchy learns, gradually, that the vocation of the hierarchy is to have authority and not power, we will come nearer to becoming what the Church is called to be: a living body, an "organism of love" — but not of sentimentality. For love is described by Christ when he says no one has greater love than those who give their lives for their neighbor.

And we speak of the structures of the Church — yes, they are a necessity. But the attitude of the people who are "in command" must be that of the servant. "I am in your midst as the one who serves," says Christ. And we are called to be servants as *he* is a servant. There are structures that are of necessity because of our frailty, because of our sinfulness, because of the temptations that the devil puts before us, because of our immaturity. But all of these should be like the Law of the Old Testament, which St. Paul calls a *paidagogos,* one who teaches, who guides.

And when we read in the beginning of Genesis that man was given dominion, we interpret it always in terms of the right to govern, to enslave, to subdue and to tread all creatures underfoot. In reality the word "dominion" in English and French comes from the Latin word *dominus,* which may mean "overlord," but can mean "teacher," "guide," or "master." Our role is to be masters guiding the whole of creation into the fullness of unity with God, not to dominate. But in this process, as I said, structures are necessary. There is need for a formal ministry.

Why a ministry at all? May I suggest — and this is my surmise, so anyone more theologically qualified than I am should put me in my place — that every human being is called to bring into the realm of God everything that surrounds him: the circumstances of life, the places, the beings. But there is one thing that cannot be done by man: he cannot sanctify himself beyond himself. We cannot by an act of will, by our own choice, become what we are not, because we have fallen away from our vocation. And this is the point at which Christ and the Holy Spirit enter into the world, become active, and commit to us two things: a sacramental ministry, that is, priests whose vocation is to bring forth to God the elements of this created world so that they can be taken out of the context of sin and brought into the context of God; and then God takes them on and sanctifies them by the strength of the Holy Spirit.

This is the essence of ministry. The administrative aspect of it is something incidental; it is not the essence. And so we find ourselves with a structured laity, a *laos,* to which the clergy belong, a clergy whose vocation is to celebrate, to perform actions — or rather to create situations in which God can act; because if you think of the Liturgy, the Liturgy *can* be celebrated and *is* celebrated by no one but Christ himself. He is the only High Priest of all creation. We can say words, we can make gestures, but the one who brings forth these gifts to God is Christ, and the power that transmutes these gifts into the Body of Christ and the Blood of Christ, that transforms the waters that we bring from the well into the waters of life eternal, is the Holy Spirit.

— *The Living Body of Christ,* 122

THE ORTHODOX DIASPORA

"Diaspora" describes accurately the state of affairs: Orthodox people of different nationalities happen to live in all the countries of the world as a religious minority, with a varying degree of scatteredness — in some places as individuals, in others as small or relatively big parishes, too distant from one another to maintain contact; in other places small or larger dioceses in the midst of much more numerous non-Orthodox bodies, always too small and also still too ethnic to be one of the denominations of the country where they live. Yet there is another dimension to being a Diaspora, a positive one. The dominant position of our Churches in the countries from which we come and their close association with the State have accustomed us to think in terms totally alien to early Christians in terms of what one often calls "the gathered community": yet the vocation of the Church is to bring the Gospel to all creatures, to be like a handful of seed that the Master of the harvest scatters far and wide, so that it bears fruit in all places where even one seed falls. Berdyaev wrote a very beautiful article on the subject in the early years of our Russian exile — telling us that we were sent by God into the whole world to bring Orthodoxy to those who had lost it and needed it; the Apostles, twelve men, and the comparatively few disciples did not stay cooped up together; they parted from one another to bring the Good News to those who sat in darkness. Though distant from each other, they knew that they were one, because they all were in Christ, and doing the work he had sent them to do. This is a true meaning of "Diaspora": to be a mission, a band of witnesses. To do this we need hardly any structures — only a keen fellowship between us all and a sincere, earnest dedication to the service of God. In this context differences of language, of culture, of ethnicity, are no impediments; they only enrich the message, make it more human, more accessible in its rich variety to all those who receive it.

It is our clinging to structures that divides us; the multiplicity of national jurisdictions would not separate us if no jurisdiction claimed superiority over others, rights of power instead of the privilege of serving more faithfully than others, if cooperation in all things was the rule. We still need bishops and clergy who speak national languages to serve those who have not yet acquired a common language with other Orthodox living in the same territory; we must cherish our languages, as both prayers, spiritual writings, and theological statements often cannot be translated adequately and need living interpreters. We must be deeply rooted in our culture in order to appreciate, assess, and share the culture of others. However, we have no right to claim any superiority for our own heritage, but a deep knowledge of it enables us to share its riches with all those who can be enriched by it.   — *The Living Body of Christ*, 184

THE CHURCH IN RUSSIA

I once spoke to Patriarch Alexis I and asked him how he would define the Church. He answered, "The Church is the Body of

Christ, crucified to save the world." I knew him fairly well and he was of course thinking of the fact that the Church is not only a body of people who are praying for the salvation of the world: we must go out into the world. Christ said to us that we are the light, that we must go into the darkness, that we are the salt, which prevents decay. We have to go there, where decay is setting in: all this provided we possess faith, that is, total assurance of the existence of God....

Russia was christened, but was not enlightened. There was a great deal of very dark faith, and a great deal of superstition — and there was also much that was golden in the Russian people. But the Church was, of course, responsible for the lack of enlightenment, the darkness, and the superstition. I say "the Church" not as the Body of Christ, but the Church as it exists in particular: you and I and all of us, and those who lived before us, and who were given the power to teach people and taught no one or taught them badly.

That is one thing. On the other hand, "The time is come that judgment must begin at the house of God" (1 Pet. 4:17). I remember that in my youth this phrase was used as proof that the Russian Church was the Church that stood above all other Churches. I think that is a very optimistic interpretation. It might have been very comforting to think so, but it was not the case.

But in reality God passed a terrible judgment on the Russian Church — and not only on the Church but also on the people. The ways of God are unfathomable. We cannot know the ways of God, we cannot know why certain things happen, but we can know where they lead. We do know that as a result of all the tragedies there came about a certain *renaissance,* a new perception of the Gospels, of Christ, of God, of the Church as something that lives and is completely new. And that is God's great mercy.   *— Encounter, 23*

THE MEANING OF TRADITION

Whenever someone dares to suggest the slightest change in the ways of the Church, he is accused of breaking with tradition. And here it is important for us to treasure tradition, but also to understand it rightly and not to become prisoners and slaves of false tradition. Tradition is something handed down to us from the very beginning, from one generation to another. But what is handed down to us is the substance and the meaning and not the form. A Russian bishop in the early years of the emigration wrote that it was not permissible to celebrate in Western languages because most heresies were born in the West — forgetting that there were enough heretics in Byzantium and elsewhere! If tradition is understood in that sense you become its prisoner. Tradition is the living memory of the Church. We all have a memory but more often than not, too often, we forget our past. The Church does not. The Church has an eternal, unshakeable memory. But memory does not mean that nothing new can enter into our experience. This memory does not force us backward at every step. It is an experience that has gradually grown into new and further experience rooted in God and inspired by the Holy Spirit. What the Church does is to look at every step of its development and its life for what St. Paul calls "the mind of Christ." To listen to the teaching of the Holy Spirit is to be always young, always new, always modern. It does not tell us to live as we lived in the twelfth century.

In a discussion with a group of Russian bishops on the ordination of women, the senior bishop articulated the following conclusion: "I have no answer on this matter, but it has not happened in the past and therefore it should never happen in the future." Whether it should happen or not is another matter. But that is not a reason. Tradition is the living memory of almost two thousand years of Christianity, living and kept alive by the action and the inspiration of the Holy Spirit and made solid, unshakeable, by the word and the person of Christ. Traditionalism is what a Roman Catholic theologian in America has described as "the dead memory that is kept by the living":

memories of things that do not exist any more in reality, that are totally useless, but that are nonetheless treasured. This is heresy. This denies the fact that the Church is alive. The Shepherd of Hermas speaks in his first vision of meeting a woman of extreme beauty with the face of a virgin and with white hair. He says to her, "Who are you?" and she answers, "I am the Church." "How is it that you are so young? You have existed for so long." She replies, "I have the youth of eternity." "But why then have you got white hair?" And the answer came: "Because I have the hair of wisdom." And this is what the Church should be. The Church is not a vague, amorphous concept. You, I, we — that is the Church. And we should have the youth of the newly born into eternity, and possess the wisdom of the centuries before us — and even more the wisdom of God that stretches into eternity. — *The Living Body of Christ*, 204

WOMEN IN THE CHURCH

Metropolitan Anthony did much to promote women in his own diocese. He not only treated them with the greatest respect, as equals (he treated everybody with respect, as equals); he also gave them roles of responsibility. Although he never went against the rules of the Church, he was not afraid to voice his thoughts on women's equality, and the rightness of female ordination.

The first selection is part of a reply to a letter sent by Syndesmos, the pan-Orthodox international youth movement, to the hierarchs of the Orthodox Churches.

I have mentioned the existence of structures of oppression creating distinctions and establishing false hierarchies of value. One is blatantly offensive and must be broken down: it is the position of women in the Church. The Orthodox Church has made more than one unwarranted statement on the subject but has not yet even begun to think about it; the problem is considered as external to us, coming from those Churches that have "lost their way." This is untrue; it is at the heart of our Church's life. It must be thought out and seen with new eyes. To be referred to the tradition is not enough, a tradition the meaning of which or whose origin cannot be traced is no tradition, but traditionalism — a superstitious survival of prejudices and misapprehensions. It is for your generation with the Gospel and the Faith given us by God in Christ to confront these evils.

— The Living Body of Christ, 188

It has taken centuries for the Church to have a coherent, acceptable, and inspiring theology of God — of the relation there is in him between nature and person, of his energies and personal being, between grace and nature; of the relation there is between God and his creatures. We should be prepared to realize that we have never given any kind of thought, leaving aside even such words as "intelligent" or "creative," to the position and situation of women in the Church.

As long as all there is to the Church is the liturgical celebration, it is easy to see that everyone is equal in a total lack of rights if he or she is a layperson, and total hegemony if he is a cleric. When it comes to the notion of the universal priesthood of all believers, we discover a form of discrimination completely contrary both to the beginning of Genesis and to the attitude of Christ, which we can deduce from the Gospels. And when we try to give a *ratio,* a *rationale,* for these things, we are told they have no *rationale* — except tradition. Perhaps we should remember the words of the American theologian Jaroslav Pelikan, who said: "Tradition is the living memory of the Church throughout the ages: Traditionalism is the dead adherence of contemporaries to what they imagine were the convictions, or faith, of their ancestors." We must rethink the problems of femininity, of womanhood and manhood, with the same earnestness we have thought out the problems of nature and person in God, of grace and nature, and so forth. And short of this we have no right to express, with the arrogance we have exhibited in the last few decades, views that I hope one day will be rejected by the whole Church.

To refer us, for example, to the person of the Mother of God and tell women that they should follow her example and be as inconspicuous as possible, is slander against the Mother of God. It is extremely poor vision. We see in the Mother of God something very different. She is not an instrument of the Incarnation. She is as totally active in it as God himself. St. Gregory Palamas says, "Without the assent of the Mother of God, the Incarnation would have been as impossible as it would have been without the positive will of God the Father."

We see in the ministry of all believers that every Christian is called to bring himself, soul and body, as a living sacrifice to God. And I remind you that the word "sacrifice" does not simply mean a blood offering, or even an offering, but an act by which something that was either profane, or profaned, becomes sacred and holy, with the Holiness of God himself.

When we think of the ministerial office, we see that that office consists in the fact that it is not only himself that the priest brings forth to God as an offering. All the Church performs is the sacrifice by the hands and voice of the priest. It is Christ's own life and death, his descent in hell, his Resurrection, his glorious Ascension, that are brought forth before the eyes of God and before the eyes of the people.

If we think of the Mother of God, tradition tells us that she was brought up into the Holy of Holies, into which the High Priest alone was allowed to enter, and this only once a year, and not otherwise than after ritual purification by blood. She, more than anyone, has brought forth the blood offering that is the sacrifice of Christ. She did this first when she brought her divine Son to the Temple to be offered to God, in accordance with the Law. And she did so when she stood silent, without a word of protest, without a cry for mercy, by the cross that brought about the death of her Son for the salvation of the world. These thoughts I want to leave with you in the context of these structures born of our narrow, at times heretical, and certainly traditionalist views of the situation of men and women.

— *The Living Body of Christ*, 218

6

Lent, Holy Week, and Easter

Metropolitan Anthony, following the Orthodox understanding of Lent and Easter, was adamant that no one could experience and celebrate the wonder of Easter without first making the journey via Calvary and coming to the foot of the cross. It was a recurrent theme in his Lenten sermons and retreat talks, many of which remain to be published.

In the Orthodox Church Easter, Pascha, is called the Feast of Feasts. It is the center of the Church's year and of the Christian's life. At the Midnight Service people stand shoulder to shoulder holding candles symbolizing the light of the Resurrection and singing the Paschal Hymn: "Christ is risen from the dead, trampling down death by death, and to those in the tombs he has given life." The priests shout "Christ is risen!" and the worshipers respond "He is risen indeed!" over and over again. It is the culmination of Christian faith, of Christian hope, indeed of our vision of heaven. The night becomes brighter than the day. We are present at the banquet of Eternity.

Yet this exuberant joy does not, cannot, stand alone. In the early Church the catechumens were baptized on Easter night just before the service, and baptism is, Orthodoxy does not forget, our being merged into Christ's death as we are submerged in the waters of the font. Only after participating in Christ's death can we rise with him to new life.

So Holy Week — and Lent (also called Great Lent or the Great Fast), which precedes it — cannot be reduced to a token observance. For forty days we must travel the hard road of the pilgrim, as Christ traveled along the roads of Palestine on his way to Jerusalem. And we must come with him to Calvary, try to understand something of the horrors of the events that culminated in his Crucifixion, and find our own place in them. That involves a very deep repentance, because it was for our sins that Christ died, and we must die to our sins as we contemplate the cross.

The Orthodox Church keeps the fasts with a strictness that has not been encountered in the Western Churches for centuries. It is not a question of giving up, but of taking on — taking on a new ascetic lifestyle, part of which is a different pattern of eating, as we revert to the vegetarian diet of the people of the Old Testament before the Flood. No animal products, olive oil, or alcohol are consumed on weekdays (olive oil and wine are taken on Saturdays and Sundays). This makes one lighter and more receptive to prayer, whether it is at home or during the long Lenten services in church. This is vitally important. We see prayer and fasting as two sides of the same coin, remembering Christ's words linking prayer and fasting (Matt. 18:21) and his own forty-day prayerful fast in the wilderness before he began his ministry.

The Lenten mood is often described as "bright sadness" or "sad brightness." It never loses sight of the joy of the Resurrection, that unconquerable joy of Christianity, while at the same time being aware of the sadness that a spiritual overhaul inevitably produces. The act of looking intently at one's life and one's relationship with God inevitably reveals how far one has fallen short of God's glorious vision for oneself. But the focus is always positive — always looking to the divine vision as the inspiration for repentance, that deep turning away of the spirit from sinfulness and back towards God. So Lent is truly a journey, a coming home to one's true self, leaving behind the baggage of worldliness and godlessness that invades us all.

Metropolitan Anthony's words on Lent, Holy Week, and Easter were spoken with this understanding in mind. His book Meditations on a Theme *is the transcription of a series of talks that look at the preparatory weeks to Great Lent, which are meant to draw us gradually into the ascetic mindset and discipline.*

A note on the Orthodox calendar: Easter and the movable feasts dependent on it are calculated according to the Julian ("Old-Style") calendar, so that it sometimes coincides with Western Easter but generally falls between one and five weeks later. The forty days of Lent are calculated slightly differently from in the West. So Orthodox Lent begins seven full weeks before Easter Sunday, on the eve of what the Greeks call Clean Monday. It ends on the eve of Lazarus Saturday (the day before Palm Sunday, when we celebrate Christ's raising of Lazarus). Palm Sunday is a feast day (when we eat fish), followed by Holy Week, which strictly speaking is not reckoned as part of the forty days of Lent but is additional to it, and is seen as its culmination. The Feast of the Annunciation often falls within Lent, in which case fish is eaten on that day.

Great Lent has a pattern that needs a little explanation. First, it is preceded by three preparatory Sundays. These gradually draw the worshiper towards the mystery of the Lenten experience, as we contemplate the longing to meet Christ, awareness of our shortcomings, and the need for a return to God. The next Sunday is called the Sunday of the Last Judgment, at which meat is eaten for the last time until Easter, and is followed by Maslenitsa, a week when we use up the last of the dairy foods (among other ways, in the cooking of pancakes) as a gradual easing into the full Lenten diet, which is completely vegan. Then follows Forgiveness Sunday, with its rite of forgiveness at the end of Vespers. The worshipers come one by one to the clergy and each other in a mutual asking of forgiveness, so that Lent is begun with past rancor and disagreements laid aside.

Each Sunday of Lent has a particular dedication: the first Sunday is known as the Triumph of Orthodoxy, and commemorates the restoration of the veneration of icons in 843. The second Sunday commemorates St. Gregory Palamas, the Orthodox saint who championed hesychasm in the fourteenth century. The remaining Sundays have a closer obvious connection to the Lenten theme: the third is called the Sunday of the cross, when we lift our eyes from our personal sinfulness to fix our attention on the Crucifixion before us. The cross gives us encouragement and strength in our Lenten effort. The fourth Sunday is dedicated to St. John Climacos, whose ascetic treatise The Ladder of Divine Ascent *is read by monastics and many lay people during the Great Fast. The fifth Sunday commemorates St. Mary of Egypt, another ascetic held up as an inspiration.*

Then follows the Saturday of the Raising of Lazarus and the Sunday of the Palms at the beginning of Holy Week itself. We have traveled the road to Jerusalem and now embark on the rigorous reliving of the events of Holy Week.

For a detailed understanding of Orthodox Lent, Father Alexander Schmemann's book Great Lent *cannot be bettered. It will enrich the experience of all Christians on their pilgrimage towards the light of Easter.*

The Lenten Endeavor — to bring a person closer to God and to his intentions for that person — is not only a journey; it is a return journey of the prodigal son from the "far country" to the Kingdom. It cannot, therefore, be anything other than a joyful journey, however difficult and strenuous it is. This is the Orthodox understanding, of which Metropolitan Anthony never tired of reminding his listeners.

Contrary to what many people think or feel, a period of spiritual endeavor (during Lent, perhaps, or while taking part in a retreat) is a time of joy because it is a time for coming home, a period when we can come back to life. It should be a time when we shake off all that is worn and dead in us in order to become able to live, and to live with all the vastness, all the depth, and all the intensity to which we are called. Unless we understand this quality of joy, we shall make of it a monstrous, blasphemous caricature, when in God's very name we make our life a misery for ourselves and for those who must pay the cost of our abortive attempts at holiness. This notion of joy coupled with strenuous effort, with ascetical Endeavor, with struggle indeed, may seem strange, and yet it runs through the whole of our spiritual life, the life of the Church and the life of the Gospel, because the Kingdom of God is to be *conquered*. It is not something simply given to those who leisurely, lazily wait for it to come. For those who would wait for it in that spirit, it will come like the Judgment of God, like the thief who takes us unawares, like the bridegroom who comes when the foolish virgins are asleep. This is not the way in which we should await the Kingdom and the Judgment. We must recapture an attitude of mind that, usually, we cannot conjure even out of our depth, something that has become strangely alien to us: the joyful expectation of the Day of the Lord — in spite of the fact that we know that this day will be a day of Judgment. It is striking to hear in church that we are proclaiming the Gospel, the gladdening news, of Judgment, but we are proclaiming that the Day of the Lord is not fear but hope and, together with the Holy Spirit, the Church can say: "Come, Lord Jesus, come quickly!" As long as we are incapable of speaking in those terms we are missing something very important in our Christian consciousness. We are still, whatever we may say, pagans dressed up in evangelical garments. We are still people for whom God is a God outside, for whom his coming is darkness and dread, whose judgment is not our redemption, but our condemnation, for whom a meeting face to face is a fearful event and not the hour we long and live for.

Unless we realize this, spiritual endeavor cannot be a joy, for it is strenuous and confronts us with judgment and responsibility — because we must judge ourselves in order to change and become able to meet the Day of the Lord, the glorious Resurrection, with an open heart, without hiding our face, ready to rejoice that he has come.   — *Meditations on a Theme,* 1

JUDGMENT: TWO PARABLES

A week before the beginning of Orthodox Lent, at the beginning of the Cheese Fast (the preparatory week when meat is not eaten but dairy foods are allowed) is the Sunday of the Last Judgment, when the fact that we shall be judged is brought to mind. Metropolitan Anthony spoke often of this, especially referring, as in this first selection, to the parable of the sheep and the goats, where Christ speaks of judgment in terms of living out one's faith in the most practical terms.

Shall I be frank? I do not like the wise virgins. I would have preferred them to give all their oil to the foolish ones, to be cast out for their sakes (Rom. 9:1–3), in a generous act of folly; but this was not the point Christ was making. His point was — "Watch!" How much of us sleep our life through? We call it day-dreaming or being imaginative. But in all truth it is slumber; reality becomes a dream, while dreams acquire cogency and our days themselves become nights and our lives sleepwalking. Besides is it not enough to close one's eyes for it to be night, for us to be entitled to sleep? Are we not all benighted! And does God not speak to our condition in the words of Isaiah (51:17): "Sleepers arise!"? Are our lights still aglow? Are we wise bridesmaids? Are those of us who find the wise virgins selfish, less selfish than they? Are we capable of awaking from our dreams, cheerful and loving, willing to sacrifice the little reality that is ours (a last glow in our sinking lamps) for others who have also been awakened by a cry in the night, but discover with horror that no reality whatsoever has survived their dreaming? Sleep, dream, unreality — is that all there is in us? Shall the Day of the Lord come upon us like a thief to rob us of all, all, all? Shall it be darkness and terror and wailing for us?

Where can we find ground for hope? Paradoxically — unexpectedly enough — in the parable of the sheep and the goats (Matt. 25:31–46).

For some unaccountable reason this parable is quoted more than any other as an image of the Judgment, a statement about its hopeless finality. Yet it tells us something essential, not about dying and doom or salvation, but about living: neither the sinners nor the just are asked anything by God about their convictions or their ritual observances; all the Lord appraises is the degree to which they have been human: "I was thirsty, and ye gave me drink: I was a stranger, and ye took me in: naked, and ye clothed me: I was sick, and ye visited me: I was in prison, and ye came unto me." Being human requires, however, imagination, a sense of humor and of occasion, and a realistic and loving concern for the true needs and wishes of the object — or shall we say the victim — of our care. Here is a story from the lives of the Desert Fathers to illustrate this point. After a full, brilliant social and political life at the court of Byzantium, St. Arsenius retired into the desert of Egypt, seeking complete solitude and contemplative silence. A lady of the court, who had been a great admirer of his, sought him out in the wilderness. She fell at his feet. "Father," she exclaimed, "I have undertaken this perilous journey to see you and hear from you just one commandment which I vow to keep all my life!" "If you truly pledge yourself never to disobey my will, here is my commandment: If you ever hear that I am in one place, go to another!" Is not this what many would say to all those do-gooders whose virtue they are doomed to endure?

To me, the point of the parable of the sheep and the goats, is this: if you have been truly and wisely human, you are ready to enter into the divine realm, to share what is God's own, as eternal life is nothing else than God's own life, shared by him with his creatures. "Having been faithful in little things, we shall be given great ones"; having been worthy of the earth, we shall be capable of living the life of heaven, partaking of the nature of God, filled with his Spirit. If we be good stewards in what was not our own (all the gifts of God) we shall come into what is our own, as is so powerfully shown in the parable of the unjust steward (Luke 16:1–12).   — *Meditations on a Theme, 97*

FORGIVENESS

Judgment would hold nothing but terror for us if we had no sure hope of forgiveness. And the gift of forgiveness itself is implicit in God's and people's love. Yet it is not enough to be granted forgiveness; we must be prepared to receive it, to accept it.

All too often forgiveness is offered, but we recoil from it: to our pride forgiveness sounds like an ultimate humiliation, and we try to eschew it by putting on false humility: "I cannot forgive myself for what I have done; how could I accept to be forgiven? I appreciate your goodness, but my conscience is too exacting, too sensitive for me to take advantage of your kindness," and it is words like "kindness" we would use, to make the gift proffered as insignificant as possible and our refusal as frustrating as we possibly can make it for our generous friend. Of course, we cannot, we should never forgive ourselves! It would be monstrous if we could; it would simply mean that we take very, very lightly the blow that we have dealt, the wound that we have inflicted, the pain, the misery, the hurt that we have caused. (And, alas! we do this whenever we are impatient at the sight of someone whom we have hurt and who seems to be pained "beyond measure." "How long are you going to sulk? Oh, stop crying! Have I not already said to you that I am sorry; what else do you want?" Such phrases mean, if translated into plain speech: "I have forgiven myself long ago; how much more am I going to wait for you to forgive me?"). God forbid that we should ever be able to forgive ourselves, but we must learn both never to allow this to happen and also to accept, to receive the free gift of another's pardon. To refuse to do so is tantamount to saying, "I do not really believe that love blots out all sins, neither do I trust in your love." We must consent to be forgiven by an act of daring faith and generous hope, welcome the gift humbly, as a miracle that love alone, love human and love divine, can work, and forever be grateful for its gratuity, its restoring healing, its reintegrating power.

One should not expect to be forgiven because one has changed for the better; neither should one make such change a condition for forgiving other people; it is only because one is forgiven, one is loved, that one can begin to change, not the other way around. And this we should never forget, although we always do.

Also we must never confuse forgiving with forgetting, or imagine that these two things go together. Not only do they not belong together, but they are mutually exclusive. To wipe out the past has little to do with constructive, imaginative, fruitful forgiveness; the only thing that must go, be erased from the past, is its venom: the bitterness, the resentment, the estrangement — but not the memory.

True forgiveness begins at the moment when the victim of injustice, of cruelty, of slander accepts the offender as he is, for no other reason than the fact that he has come back, like the prodigal son whose father asked no questions, made no claims, set no conditions for his reintegration into the household. God's forgiveness is ours from the moment when God takes upon himself the burden and all the consequences of our fall, when the Son of God becomes the Man of Sorrows (Isa. 52–53). It is emphatically not when we become a saint! God has already granted forgiveness when he has said: "I am ready to die for you: I love you." This is also where forgiveness begins between human persons. If in a family crisis the offender simply comes back, too proud or too shy, or perhaps too cramped by fear, to say much, his redemption begins at the very moment when his family say to him: "But we never ceased to love you; let go of your fear; we still love you — oh, the pain of it! Now that you are back we shall all be healed." And this, the person who is *right* can do and should do, because it is so much easier for him to do than for the person who is in the wrong; also because those who are right share with the offenders the responsibility of the rift, of the quarrel, and must atone for it also. Theirs must be the first steps towards reconciliation. I remember a man of some standing who once came to see me and told me that a friend of his who claimed no small spiritual achievements had offended him: "Who should go and make his peace with the other?" he asked. "I cannot answer your question," I replied, "as I cannot possibly set myself as a judge between you, but one thing is certain to me: the meanest of the two of you will wait for the other to make the move." The great man said no word, but went forthwith to make his peace with his friend. Vanity had done what neither humility, nor wisdom, nor even simple friendship had been able to achieve. How sad...How different was the generous, loving, free forgiveness that the Father granted his prodigal son!

Yet in neither case was forgiveness the end of all problems: in the faraway, strange country of dereliction, the rejected offender cannot but have learned ways that are repellent to his family and friends: the smell of the swine may well still cling to the body of the prodigal son, and the habits of his wayward life will not vanish overnight; he will have to unlearn them gradually, possibly very slowly; he is bound to have lost many of the more refined manners of his original surroundings; he will have to learn them again, slowly. And the family will be able to reintegrate, to regenerate and redeem him only to the extent to which its members will remember (not forget) his weaknesses, the flaws in his character, the bad habits acquired by him. But remember without resentment, without a feeling of superiority, without a feeling of shame, but with the pain of compassion, with that compassion that makes "grace abound where sin is present"; with the will and a stern determination never to forget what there is that the beloved one should be shielded from — his natural frailty, his acquired weakness. Otherwise he who needs our healing and protecting help will be submitted to overwhelming temptation and become the victim of never-ending, bitter recrimination. To forgive and to put under probation are two very different things. To forgive means to accept the other "as Christ has received us," to "bear one another's burdens" as he bears ours, simultaneously those of the victim and of the offender, loving joyfully, gratefully, the victim, loving the offender sacrificially, with the joy of self-offering.

This is God's way. His cross witnesses to his faith in mankind and in every single man, his unconquerable hope; this is why his death becomes our life, and his Resurrection — Eternity itself for us. *— Meditations on a Theme,* 104

FORGIVENESS SUNDAY

We are now on our journey from the land of dereliction to the glorious land, where we meet the Loving God as children of his Kingdom. The Church at this moment is an apt image of the situation in which we are; we are in twilight, and we see the sanctuary of God, God's own realm in all the glory of light. And yet we know that Christ has brought light into the world, that he is the Light, and that we are children of Light. It is from darkness to twilight and from the twilight into the full glory of the uncreated Light of God that we are now moving. As in every journey, when one leaves the place of one's habitual abode, one is still full of feelings and memories and impressions; and then gradually they fade away until in the end nothing is left but the expectation of the end of our journey....

And so, in the course of this week let us for the last time look at ourselves and look at one another and make our peace. Making peace, reconciliation, does not mean that all problems are over. Christ came into the world to reconcile the world with himself and in him with God; we know what it cost him: he gave himself, helpless, vulnerable, unprotected, gave himself to us, saying: Do with me what you want, and when you will have done your worst, see that my love has never faltered, and that it could be joy and it could be searing pain, but it was nothing but love....

And this is an example that we can, that we must follow if we want to be Christ's own people. Forgiveness comes at the moment when we say to one another: I recognize your frailty, I see how deeply you wound me, and because I am wounded, because I am a victim — at times guilty, and at times inno-cent — I can turn to God, and from the depth of pain and of agony, of shame, and at times of despair, I can say to the Lord: Lord — forgive! He does not know what he is doing! If he only knew how deeply wounding his words are, if he only knew how destructive he is for me in my life, he would not do it. But he is blind, he is immature, he is frail; and I accept his frailty, and I will carry him, or her, as a good shepherd carries the lost sheep;

because we are all lost sheep of the fold of Christ. Or else, if necessary, I will carry him, or her, or them as Christ carried his cross — to the point of death, to the point of love crucified, to the point when all power of forgiveness is given if we only have accepted to forgive whatever was done to us.

And so let us enter into this Lent, as one moves from darkness into twilight, and from twilight into light: with joy and light in our hearts, shaking off our feet the dust of the earth, shaking off all the fetters that make us prisoners — prisoners of greed, of envy, of fear, of hatred, of jealousy, prisoners of our lack of mutual understanding, prisoners of our self-centeredness because we live like prisoners within ourselves and we are called by God to be free. Then we will see how step after step we move as though it were across the vast sea, away from the earth of darkness and twilight towards the divine light, we will meet the Crucifix, and we will meet one day at the end of it love divine revealed to us in its tragic perfection before it reaches us as an unutterable glory and joy. First, Passion Week, first the cross; and then the wonder of Resurrection. We must enter into both, enter into the Passion of Christ together with him, and enter together with him into the great peace and into the shining light of the Resurrection.

For myself, I will ask forgiveness of you for all that I have not done that should have been done, for the awkward way in which I do things, and for the many, many things that should be done and are never done.

But let us now support one another on this journey by mutual forgiveness, by love, remembering that very often on a hard journey it is the people from whom we expect nothing good that at a moment of crisis will stretch out a supportive hand — people whom we thought were alien to us, or inimical, who suddenly will see our need and meet it. So let us open our hearts, our minds and eyes and be ready to see and to respond.

Let us now begin by going to the icon of Christ, our God and our Savior, who paid a heavy price to have power to forgive; let us turn to the Mother of God who has given her only begotten

Son for our salvation; if she can forgive — who would refuse forgiveness to us?

And then turn to one another. While we come we will hear no longer songs of repentance, but as though they were coming from afar off, the hymns of the Resurrection that will grow stronger halfway to the Feast of the cross, and will fill this church and indeed the world in the night when Christ was raised and his victory won. Amen.

— Sermon at Vespers, Forgiveness Sunday, March 16, 1986

ST. GREGORY PALAMAS SUNDAY

Last week we kept the day of the Triumph of Orthodoxy, the day when the Church proclaimed that it was legitimate and right to paint icons of Christ; it was not a declaration about art; it was a deeply theological proclamation of the Incarnation. The Old Testament said to us that God cannot be represented by any image because he was bottomless mystery; he had even no Name except the mysterious name that only the High Priest knew. But in the New Testament we have learned and we know from experience that God has become man, that the fullness of the Godhead has abided and is still abiding forever in the flesh; and therefore God has a human name, Jesus, and he has a human face that can be represented in icons. An icon is therefore a proclamation of our certainty that God has become man; and he has become man to achieve ultimate, tragic, and glorious solidarity with us, to be one of us that we may be one of the children of God.

And today we remember the name of St. Gregory Palamas, one of the great saints of Orthodoxy, who against heresy and doubt, proclaimed from within the experience of the ascetics and of all believers, that the grace of God is not a created Gift — it is God himself, communicating himself to us so that we are pervaded by his presence, that we gradually, if we only receive him, open ourselves to him, become transparent or at least translucent to his light, that we become incipiently and ever increasingly partakers of the divine nature.

This is not simply a promise; this is a certainty that we have because this has happened to thousands and thousands of men and women whom we venerate as the saints of God: they have become partakers of the divine nature; they are to us a revelation and certainty of what we are called to be and become.

And today one step more brings us into the joy, the glory of Easter. Amen!

— From a sermon on the Sunday of St. Gregory Palamas, Second Sunday of Lent, March 11, 1990

SUNDAY OF THE CROSS

In today's Gospel the Lord says to us that if we want to be followers of his, disciples, we must take up our crosses and follow him. And when we think of the cross of the Lord, we think of his gradual, painful ascent to his Crucifixion, we think of the way of the cross, of his death. And indeed, the Lord calls us, if we want to be faithful to him, if we want to be his disciples, to be prepared to walk all the way with him — all the way.

But on the other hand, we must remember that he does not call us to follow a road that he has not trod himself. He is a Good Shepherd who walks ahead of his sheep, making sure that all is clear, that dangers have been removed, that they can walk safely in his footsteps.

His call to take up our cross and to follow him is a call, at the same time, to accept being true disciples of him, and also to do it in the certainty that he will never ask from us what he has not done or endured himself. We can follow him safely; we can follow him with assurance, but also with a sense of peace in our heart and our mind.

And yet this following is not devoid of tragedy because to be disciples of Christ we must, as the reading of the Epistle at our baptism warned us, die with him in order to be risen with him.

To die means to renounce, in an act of loyalty, of friendship, of solidarity with him, of respect and veneration for him, of recognition of the cost to him for his love of us, to renounce everything that was the cause of his death. We must reflect on everything within us that makes us alien to God, unworthy of ourselves, unworthy of his love.

And when we discover this, whatever it may be, we must set out to reject it from our lives. It may be things that seem to be easy, or small, it may be things that are very heavy and difficult to reject. But we must not imagine that things that seem to be small things separate us less from God than those things that appear to be great to us. There is a story in the life of one of the ascetics to whom two persons came; the one had committed a grievous sin and the other one recognized only a multitude of little sins. And to make them understand that both matter and each could be as destructive of life as the other, he told the first one to go into the field and to find the biggest boulder to be found and bring it, and to the other one to collect pebbles, everywhere. The one easily found a boulder and brought it; the other one as easily found a multitude of little pebbles. And when they came back, he said to them, "Now go, and put them back exactly where you found them. The first, who brought the big boulder, easily found the place; it was deeply imprinted in the earth, and he placed the boulder exactly where it had lain. The other one, after hours and hours and hours came back with all the pebbles, because they had been collected at random, and it was impossible to remember where. So it is with our sins: there is nothing that is small, and there is nothing that is great, if — and the "if" is important — if we do not find a way of putting it aside.

...And now, we are going to see one after the other what the grace of God accepted, heroically received, can make of people: in the person of St. John of the Ladder, in the person of St. Mary of Egypt, in the person of every sinner who is remembered in these weeks, and who by the power and the grace and the love of God, but also by his heroic, wholehearted, sincere response proved capable of receiving what God was giving.

And then we will come to Holy Week; and from the light that has shone as a promise, dimly or brightly in the saints, we will see the blinding light of love divine incarnate, of what God means when he says that he loves us. And again, it is judgment, because if men, women, children as frail as we are could respond as the saints did, what are we going to say to God if we respond in no manner to his own sacrificial, crucified love?

And so, from the twilight of sin revealed to us, to the light which has shone through the saints and in the saints, of the divine grace, we come to the light pure, perfect, revealed in God, and at each stage we are told by God: Are you going to respond to this? Is the horror of darkness not sufficient to make you shudder? Is the vision of what can be done not enough to inspire you? Is my own life and death for your sake not sufficient to move you? We are given one chance after the other to change, to respond: Let us do it! Let us make haste to do it!

And so we can enter into these days with hope, because one sigh of the publican was enough to make him a child of the Kingdom, to restore him to wholeness. Let us bring at least one sigh from the depth of our heart — and salvation is ours....
Glory be to God, Glory be to God in all things. Amen.

— From a sermon, Sunday of the Cross, April 2, 1989

PALM SUNDAY AND HOLY WEEK

Today on the day of Palms we stand in awe and amazement before what is happening — in a way in which the Jews of Jerusalem could not meet Christ; because they met him imagining that he was the glorious king who would now take over all power, conquer and reject the heathen, the Romans who were occupying their country, that he would reestablish a kingdom, an earthly kingdom of Israel. We know that he had not come for that; he had come to establish a Kingdom that will have no end, a Kingdom of eternity, and the Kingdom that was not open

only to one nation but was open to all nations, and the Kingdom that was to be founded on the life and on the death of
Jesus Christ, the Son of God become the Son of man.

And Holy Week is from one end to another a time of tragic
confusion. The Jews meet Christ at the gates of Jerusalem
because they expect of him a triumphant military leader. And
he comes to serve, to wash the feet of his disciples, to give his
life for the people — but not to conquer by force, by power. And
the same people who meet him shouting, "Hosanna to the Son
of David" in a few days will shout, "Crucify him, crucify him!"
because he has betrayed their expectations. They expected an
earthly victory, and what they see is a defeated king. They hate
him for the disappointment of all their hopes.

And this is not so alien to us in our days. How many are
those people who have turned away in hatred from Christ
because he has disappointed one hope or another. I remember
a woman who had been a believer for all her life and whose
grandson died, a little boy. And she said to me, "I don't believe
in God anymore. How could he take my grandson?" And I said
to her, "But you believed in God while thousands and thousands and millions of people died." And she looked at me and
said, "Yes, but what did that do to me? I didn't care, they were
not my children." This is something that happens to us in a
small degree so often. We waver in our faith and in our faith-
fulness to God when something that we expect him to do for
us is not done, when he is not an obedient servant; when we
proclaim our will he does not say, "Amen," and does not do it.
So we are not so alien from those who met Christ at the gates
of Jerusalem and then turned away from him.

But we are entering now into Holy Week. How can we
face the events? I think we must enter into Holy Week not
as observers, not reading the passages of the Gospel that are
relevant. We must enter into Holy Week as though we were
participants in the events, indeed read of them but then mix in
the crowd that surrounds Christ and ask ourselves, Who am
I in this crowd? Am I one of those who said, "Hosanna to
the Son of David!"? And am I now on the fringe of saying,

"Crucify him"? Am I one of the disciples who were faithful until the moments of ultimate danger came upon them? You remember that in the Garden of Gethsemane three disciples had been singled out for Christ to support him at the hour of his supreme agony, and they did not. They were tired, they were despondent, and they fell asleep. Three times he came to them for support; three times denied it.

We do not meet Christ in the same circumstances, but we meet so many people who are in agony, not only dying physically — and that also happens to our friends, our relatives, people around us — but are in agony of terror one way or another. Are we there awake, alive, attentive to them, ready to help them out, and if we can't help, to be with them, to stand by them? Or do we fall asleep, that is, turn away, leave them in their agony, their fear, their misery? And again I am not speaking of Judas, because none of us is aware of betraying Christ in such a way; but don't we betray Christ when we turn away from all his commandments, when he says, "I give you an example for you to follow," and we shake our heads and say, "No, I will simply follow the devices of my own heart"? But think of Peter, apparently the strongest, the one who spoke time and again in the name of others, when it came to risking his life — not his life, to be rejected simply, because no one was about to kill him — he denied Christ three times.

What do we do when we are challenged in the same way, when we are in danger of being mocked and ridiculed and put aside by our friends or our acquaintances who shrug their shoulders and say, "Christian? And you believe in that? And you believe that Christ was God, and you believe in his Gospel, and you are on his side?" How often? Oh, we don't say, "No, we are not"; but do we say, "Yes, it is my glory, and if you want to crucify him, if you want to reject him, reject me too, because I choose to stand by him, I am his disciple, even if I am to be rejected, even if you don't let me into your house anymore."

And think of the crowd on Calvary. There were people who had been instrumental in his condemnation; they mocked him, and they had won their victory, so they thought at least. And then there were the soldiers, the soldiers who crucified him. They had crucified innumerable other people; they were doing their job. It didn't matter to them whom they crucified. And yet Christ prayed for them, "Forgive them, Father, they don't know what they are doing." We are not being crucified physically, but do we say, "Forgive, Father, those who offend us, who humiliate us, who reject us, those who kill our joy and darken our life in us"? Do we do that? No, we don't. So we must recognize ourselves in them also.

And then there was a crowd of people who had poured out of the city to see a man die, the fierce curiosity that pushes so many of us to be curious when suffering, agony, comes upon people. You will say, it doesn't happen. Ask yourself how you look at television and how eagerly, hungrily you look at the horrors that befall Somalia, the Sudan, Bosnia, and every other country. Is it with a broken heart? Is it that you can *not* endure the horror, and turn in prayer to God and then give, give, give generously all you can give for hunger and misery to be alleviated? Is it? No, we are the same people who came out on Calvary to see a man die. Curiosity, interest? Yes, alas.

And then there were those who had come with the hope that he would die because if he died on the cross, then they were free from this terrifying, horrible message he had brought that we must love one another to the point of being ready to die for each other. That message of crucified, sacrificial love could be rejected once and for all if he who preached it died and it was proved that he was a false prophet, a liar.

And then there were those who had come in the hope that he would come down from the cross, and then they could be believers without any risk, they would have joined the victorious party. Aren't we like that so often?

And then there is a point to which we hardly should dare turn our eyes. The Mother of the Incarnate Son of God, the Mother of Jesus — silent, offering his death for the salvation of mankind, silent and dying with him hour after hour; and the disciple who knew in a youthful way how to love his master, standing by in horror, seeing his Master die and the Mother in agony. Are we like this when we read the Gospel? Are we like this when we see the agony of men around us?

Let us therefore enter into this Holy Week in order not to be observers of what happened then. Let us enter into it mixed with the crowd and at every step ask ourselves: Who am I in this crowd? Am I the Mother? Am I the disciple? Am I one of the crucifiers? And so forth. And then we will be able to meet the day of the Resurrection together with those to whom it was life and resurrection indeed, when despair had gone, new hope had come, God had conquered. Amen.

— From a sermon, Palm Sunday, April 4, 1993

THE RESURRECTION AND THE CROSS

We must at no moment forget that the end of our journey is our meeting with the Risen Christ....Let us now turn to this event of the Resurrection to ask ourselves why it is so central, why St. Paul could say, "If Christ was not raised we are of all men the most miserable, for our faith is vain." Indeed, if Christ was not raised, our whole faith, all our conviction, our inner life, our hope, all is founded on a lie, all is founded on something that never took place and that cannot serve as the foundation for anything.

Let us now think, separately, of St. Paul and of the twelve Apostles. St. Paul, as you know, Hebrew of the Hebrews, pupil of the greatest teachers, a man of burning faith, grounded in the Scriptures, passionately faithful to the tradition of his fore-fathers, St. Paul who could have met Christ, St. Paul who certainly was in contact with Christ's disciples, St. Paul who left nothing undone in order to know, to understand, and to judge this new prophet — comparing all he knew of him with all he had understood in Holy Scripture and in the witness of the Hebraic tradition — St. Paul had rejected Christ. With all that he believed about the coming Messiah, he had not been able to recognize the Messiah when he came. It was with the intention of destroying the first seeds of the Christian faith that he had left Jerusalem and was on the way to Damascus; and it was on this journey, the journey of a persecutor, that he found himself face to face with the Risen Christ. And it is this meeting that gave absolute meaning and value to all that he had hitherto denied; having encountered the Risen Christ he knew with an immediate, blinding conviction that he who had died on the cross, whom he had refused to recognize as the Messiah, was in truth the one whom Israel awaited.

Because Christ was risen, alive in front of him after a real death, he was able to recognize that all that Christ had spoken of himself and all that was mysterious and unexplained in Scripture regarding the coming Messiah was true and concerned the Prophet of Galilee. And it is in the light of this Resurrection that the entire faith of the Gospel became possible for him and for many others. It is only because of the Resurrection that one can recognize the Son of God in him who died on the cross, and that we can receive, with conviction and certitude, the total Gospel story beginning with the Annunciation, the Virgin Birth, the teaching, the miracles, and the witness of Christ concerning himself, corroborated by the witness of God on behalf of his Christ.

This is enough, perhaps, for us to grasp one of the essential aspects of the Resurrection and its importance, but if we now turn to the Twelve, we see that the Resurrection had an even greater meaning, if such were possible. The death of Christ on the cross was something far greater and more basic in the experience of the Apostles than the death of a friend, a master, and a leader. They did more than mourn the loss of a beloved friend, the defeat of a leader they had believed would triumph. If we read the Gospel attentively, from the point of view of the relation that existed between the Apostles and the Lord, we see how, little by little, an identification grows between the Master and his disciples. Having come to him, some in an act of faith, others skeptically ("Can any good thing come out of Nazareth?" John 1:46), having passed through all the vicissitudes of hesitation and of doubt, and being completely won not only by what Christ preached but by his whole personality, we see them, before the Crucifixion, forming a group that can really be described as separated from the world, elect in the sense of "chosen and redeemed." Christ had become their absolute center of life. When Christ addressed his disciples and asked them if they also wished to leave him, Peter replied, "Lord, to whom shall we go? Thou hast the words of eternal life." Here we have a human group, centered around someone who is eternal life made manifest in a transitory, ephemeral world, the world into which human sin introduces death and corruption; and this human group cannot exist apart from this relation to Christ, not because they are tied by affection, friendship, loyalty, but because in him they have already the experience of eternal life, of a new dimension, a dimension not of relationship, but ontological, substantial. It is not just a life greater, fuller, richer, more beautiful; it is a different life that Christ has brought them.

And when Christ died on the cross, rejected, betrayed by those who stayed outside this circle of love, this mystery of divine, present, incarnate, active, transfiguring love, it is not just a question of the death of a friend and master; it is a far greater tragedy. If it were possible for Christ, with all that he represented, to die upon the cross, this meant that human hatred was stronger than divine love; human hatred had managed to repulse divine love, to banish him from the habitations of man, had rejected him and killed him on Calvary. And this death of divine love, this rejection, is accompanied by the loss, also, of the presence of eternal life in the midst of mankind: it has been cast out. Divine love, which had been offered to man in such a way as to be both a reproach and a great hope, this divine love is rejected, and without it, what remains to man? Just that which was always theirs, twilight in which to struggle, separated from Christ, a twilight consisting of a little affection, a little hatred, and plenty of indifference, a twilight in which men are strangers to one another, where relations are fragile, held together by ties that break repeatedly, by attachments that disengage and dissolve.

But what of those men who were united to Christ, who had experienced the presence of the Living God in their midst? All that remained was the possibility of enduring, of continuing to exist, but no more to live. Since they had tasted eternal life, the ephemeral life of time that ends in corruption and death was no more than a prospect of the final defeat, a postponement of the return to dust — that which could no longer be called life but was a "predeath." So that when Scripture by means of images or direct words makes us understand that in the death of Christ we are all dead, to the degree that we are profoundly identified and allied to him, and that in his Resurrection we come back to life with him, Scripture is speaking to us of something very precise and real. But there is here something that we cannot grasp with the same tragic darkness as that which filled the Apostles, and for a very simple and obvious reason, namely, that on Good Friday, whatever effort of imagination we make to dwell only on the tragedy, we know precisely, that before the end of three days we shall be singing of the Resurrection. We cannot obliterate our knowledge of Christ's Resurrection: not only because year after year we have experienced it, and we cannot artificially forget it, but because as members of the Body of Christ, as Christians integrated into the mystery of Christ — the total Christ that is the Church — we have within us this eternal life that witnesses to the fact that the darkness of Good Friday is already overcome; within us it is already overcome, within us the light is already present, life is already present, victory, partially at least, is already won. And for us it is impossible not to remember the coming Resurrection although we are in the midst of Good Friday.

But for the Apostles, Good Friday was the last day of the week and the last day of life as they had known it; on the following day, the day that preceded the Resurrection, the darkness was as dense, as obscure, as impenetrable as it had been on Good Friday; and if the Resurrection had not happened, all the days of the year and all the days of their life would have been days of total darkness, days when God was dead, when God had been conquered, when God had been definitely and radically exiled from the community of men. And if you bear in mind the unity that was gradually created between Christ and his disciples, so that the life they lived was his life — in him and through him they moved, saw, perceived, and understood — you will grasp that his death was not only this total and irremediable darkness of Good Friday — for them the last day of history — but it was also their own death because Life had been taken away from them; they could no longer live but merely exist.

Thus you will understand why for the Apostles the Resurrection was such a complete renewal, such a decisive event: when Christ, on the third day, appeared to them, all the doors being shut, their first thought was that it was a hallucination, an apparition. And Christ on that occasion, as on all the occasions of his appearance after the Resurrection related in the Gospel, insisted on the fact that he was not a ghost, not an illusion, but a true corporeal presence. He shares food with them. And we also understand why Christ's first words are words of peace. "Peace be unto you!" He brings them the peace that had been taken from them by his death, which was their death; he released them from the utter, hopeless confusion in which they were submerged, this twilight state wherein life was unrecognizable, this transitory life from whence Eternity had been driven; and he gave them that peace which he had promised, that peace which only he could give, that "peace which passeth all understanding," the peace of reintegration into life, beyond all doubt, beyond all hesitation — the certainty possessed by men who, because they are alive, cannot doubt Life, the life of the world to come, already come, by means of Christ's Resurrection and the gift of the Holy Spirit.   — *Meditations on a Theme*, 111

GOOD FRIDAY

Let us go . . . to Good Friday, the day when Christ died upon the cross that we may live. A Russian hymn says:

> O *Life Eternal, how is it that Thou art brought to the grave,*
> O *Light, how is it that Thou art quenched?*

Indeed it is life eternal that seems to go down to the grave. It is light eternal, the glory of God revealed to us in his Son that seems to be quenched, to be removed from us forever. To understand the meaning of Good Friday, of the saving death of Christ, we must understand the meaning of the Incarnation. Each of us is born into time out of nonbeing. We enter a fleeting, precarious life in order to grow into the stability of eternal life. Eternity is God himself, whom we can meet in the ephemeral flow of time and through this meeting, through the communion that God offers us by grace and love in mutual freedom, we can also enter into eternity to share God's own life, become in the daring words of St. Peter "partakers of the divine nature."

The birth of the Son of God is unlike ours. He does not enter time out of naught. His birth is not the beginning of life, of an ever-growing life; it is a limitation of the fullness that was his before the world began. He who possessed eternal glory with the Father before all ages, enters into our world, into the created world, wherein man has brought sin, suffering, death. Christ's birth is for him not the beginning of life; it is the beginning of death. He accepts all that is inherent in our condition and the first day of his life on earth is the first day of his ascent to the cross.

His death has a quality, a weight, that belongs to him alone. We are not saved by the death of Christ because it was particularly cruel. Countless men, women, and children throughout the ages have suffered as cruelly. Many have burnt in flames, many have frozen in ice, many have died of long, excruciatingly painful illness, many have suffered torture and imprisonment in camps in the horrors of war. The death of Christ is unique because Jesus of Nazareth could not die. It is not his Resurrection that is the incredible miracle. It is his death. We know from the writings of St. Paul, from the faith indeed of the whole

Church, that death is the result of sin, sin being understood as our severance from our communion with God. And Christ is God himself incarnate. United to his Godhead, his very humanity, his true humanity, is beyond death. The incarnate Son of God makes his very flesh, his very human nature incorruptible and beyond dying. And yet he dies. Here lies the paradox and here is the tragedy, the tragedy unequalled. One of the saints of the Orthodox Church tells us that in the Incarnation of Christ two events take place. On the one hand, he becomes man, but he reveals to us the real humanity to which we are called — a humanity rooted in the divine life itself, inseparable from God, unconquerable by death. But to become one of us, to share with us truly, our suffering and our dereliction, Christ takes upon himself all the crushing weight of the human condition, all the limitations that otherwise are alien to his glorious humanity: the pain and the weariness, hunger and thirst, and the very possibility of death, and when the hour comes, he dies our death upon the cross, but a death that is more than ours. We die because we die out, our body decays and falls away, we can no longer live. If in the course of this transitory life we have acquired the knowledge of God, a common life with him, then dying no longer means for us a defeat but a new abundance and fullness of life, as St. Paul sees it when he says that for him to die does not consist in losing life, but of being clad, vested in the life of eternity. But dying is always a tragedy for us; body and soul are parted, the completeness of the human being is broken up and we must wait for the Resurrection of the body and the victory of life eternal to become truly, fully, what we are called to be.

But in the death of Christ something different happens. He dies although he cannot die; he dies although he is immortal, in his very human nature inseparably united with his Godhead. His soul, without being separated from God, is torn out of his body, while both his soul and his flesh remain united with the Godhead. He will lie in the tomb incorruptible until the third day, because his body cannot be touched by corruption. It is full of the divine presence. It is pervaded by it as a sword of iron is pervaded by fire in the furnace, and the soul of Christ descends into hell resplendent with the glory of his Godhead. The death of Christ is a tearing apart of an immortal body from a soul that is alive and remains alive forever. This makes the death of Christ a tragedy beyond our imagining, far beyond any suffering that we can humanly picture or experience. Christ's death is an act of supreme love. It was true when he said, "No one takes my life from me; I give it freely myself." No one could kill him — the Immortal; no one could quench this Light that is the shining of the splendor of God. He gave his life, he accepted the impossible death to share with us all the tragedy of our human condition.   — *Meditations on a Theme*, 120

Christ, in his acceptance of the human situation, has identified himself with us, not only in our stability but also in our frailty and in our misery. He was abandoned, lonely, hated, despised, and so forth; that is also true. He accepted the company of people whose company others didn't want — the sinners, those who were despised; that is also true. But there is something more in the way in which he accepts solidarity with us, and something much more important. He accepts solidarity with us *in death*. One says, quite naturally: he chose to become a man, so he had to die of it. No he hadn't, and this is just the point. A number of writers have pointed out that death can be conceivable only through severance from the source of life. One cannot be, as it were, plugged into life eternal and die. St. Maxim the Confessor underlines the fact that at the moment of his conception, at the moment of his birth, in his humanity Christ had no participation in death, because his humanity was pervaded with the eternal life of his divinity. He could not die. It is not an allegory or a metaphor when in the Orthodox Church on Thursday in Holy Week, we sing, "O Life Eternal, how can you die; O Light, how can you be quenched?"

This is a point that I think we should consider.

He died on the cross, and the operative words are the most tragic words of history. He, who is the Son of God, because he has accepted total, final, unreserved, and unlimited solidarity with men in all their conditions, without participation in evil but accepting all its consequences; he, nailed on the cross, cries out the cry of forlorn humanity, "My God, my God, why hast Thou forsaken me?"

People who are keen on exegesis explain to us that at that point he was rehearsing a verse of a prophetic song. It you have seen anyone die a violent death you can't well imagine him at the last moment rehearsing a prayer he had been taught when he was a little boy! Besides, it is an error of vision — for it is a prophecy that is turned towards its fulfillment, not fulfillment that is supposed to recite words of prophecy. No, it was something real. When Christ said "My God, my God, why hast Thou forsaken me?" He was crying out, shouting out the words of a humanity that had lost God, and he was participating in that very thing which is the only real tragedy of humanity — all the rest is a consequence. The loss of God is death, is forlornness, is hunger, is separation. All the tragedy of man is in one word, "Godlessness." And he participates in our godlessness, not in the sense in which we reject God, but in a more tragic way, in a way in which one can lose what is the dearest, the holiest, the most precious, the very heart of one's life and soul. And when in the Apostles' Creed, we repeat, "And he descended into hell," we very often think "That's one of those expressions," and we think of Dante and of the place where all those poor people are being tortured with such inventiveness by God.

But the hell of the Old Testament has nothing to do with this spectacular hell of Christian literature. The hell of the Old Testament is something infinitely more horrid; it is the place where God is not. It's the place of final dereliction, it's the place where you continue to exist and there is no life left. And when we say that he descended into hell, we mean that having accepted the loss of God, to be one of us in the only major tragedy of that kind, he accepted also the consequences and goes to the place where God is not, to the place of final dereliction; and there, as ancient hymns put it, the gates of hell open to receive him who was unconquered on earth, and who now is conquered, a prisoner, and they receive this man who has accepted death in an immortal humanity, and Godlessness without sin, and they are confronted with the divine presence because he is both man and God, and hell is destroyed. There is no place left where God is not. And the old prophetic song is fulfilled: "Where shall I flee from Thy face — in heaven is Thy throne, in hell [understood in Hebrew — the place where you are not], you are also." This is the measure of Christ's solidarity with us, of his readiness to identify himself, not only with our misery but with our godlessness. If you think of that, you will realize that there is not one atheist on earth who has ever plunged into the depths of godlessness as the Son of God, become the Son of Man, has done. He is the only one to know what it means to be without God and to die of it.   — *God and Man,* 54

The joy of the Resurrection is something that we, too, must learn to experience, but we can experience it only if we first learn the tragedy of the cross. To rise again we must die. Die to our hampering selfishness, die to our fears, die to everything that makes the world so narrow, so cold, so poor, so cruel. Die so that our souls may live, may rejoice, may discover the spring of life. If we do this then the Resurrection of Christ will have come down to us also. But without the death on the cross there is no Resurrection, the Resurrection that is a joy, the joy of life recovered, the joy of the life that no one can take away from us anymore! The joy of a life that is superabundant, that like a stream runs down the hills, carrying with it heaven itself reflected in its sparkling waters. The Resurrection of Christ is reality in history as his death on the cross was real, and it is because it belongs to history that we believe in it. It is not only with our hearts but with the totality of our experience that we know the risen Christ. We can know him day by day as the Apostles knew him. Not the Christ of the flesh, not Christ as he was seen in bewilderment by people who surrounded him in the days of his earthly life, but the everliving Christ, the Christ of the spirit of whom St. Paul speaks, the risen Christ who belongs to time and eternity because he died once upon the cross but lives forever. The Resurrection of Christ is the one, the only event that belongs both to the past and to the present.

To the past because it did happen, on a given day, in a given place, at a given moment, because it was seen and known as an event in time, in the life of those who had known him. But it belongs also to every day because Christ, once risen, is ever alive, and each of us can know him personally, and unless we know him personally we have not yet learned what it means to be a Christian.   *— Meditations on a Theme,* 119

EASTER

The Feast of the Resurrection of Christ is the beginning of newness, of a life that no longer fears death, a life that is stronger than death, a life that can face death in the way in which St. Paul spoke of it when he said that for him to die is not to divest himself of temporary life, but to clothe himself with eternity! The measure of the love of God for us is all the life, all the teaching, but also all the death of Christ who died for us; and the measure he gives for perfect love is that no one can have a greater love than he or she who is prepared to give his life for his neighbor. And this neighbor may be a friend, but he also may be a foe! St. Paul insisted on it when he says that Christ gave his life not only for those who received him, accepted him as their Lord, followed him whithersoever he chose to go, but also for those who remained his enemies; and for them he prayed, and he commands us by his example and his word to pray the same prayer for those who hate us, who persecute us: Forgive them, Father, they don't know what they are doing....

But in the Incarnation we have a new vision of man: man is vast enough, deep enough to unite himself to God — the fullness of God abided is the flesh, and we are called to be a revelation not only in words, but in our life, in our persons of this miracle of the greatness of man! But to be great is costly, and at times frightening: we must put our trust in God, and accept to be so great as one day to become, according to the daring words of St. Peter, partakers of the divine nature. And we must believe in man as no unbeliever can believe in man, believe in the greatness of man, in the vastness, in the holiness, the prospective holiness of man! And together with all believers and unbelievers, the persecutors and the friends, build such a city of man that it should be as great, as vast, as holy as the City of God of whom the first Citizen could be the Lord Jesus Christ! Isn't that a vocation great enough, holy enough, isn't it worth living and dying for this — to make of our earth the Kingdom of God? Let us therefore, in the certainty that Christ has overcome all evil, has overcome mortality and death, has overcome all the powers of destruction — let us build this city at the cost of our lives, but also in the glory of God! Amen.   — Easter sermon (undated)

EASTER SERMON

Christ is life and the victory of life. In the world in which he came, death was prevalent and seemed to be all-powerful over men; when he came, he defeated death by his Resurrection. And nowadays we live in a world full of torment, of pain, of fear, of murder, of death, and we may say: but where is the victory? The victory is in each of us, the victory is in all those of us who believe that death cannot separate us from God, that death is no longer a victory of evil over us, but a triumph of us through our faith, because death is no longer separation. St. Paul says that for him death is a meeting with Christ; as long as he lives in the flesh he is separated, partly, from God. But with his death he enters in full unity and communion with him. This is our faith, but there is more to it in a sense, because life is triumphant in our midst. However frightening and dark the world is nowadays, we know that victory has already been won, that God has won and that we who believe in him partake together with him in his victory. And therefore, let us bring, to all around us, this message of life and glory!

Christ is risen!   — Easter sermon, April 11, 1999

Epilogue

Metropolitan Anthony spent his life bringing the Gospel to people, and people to God. He did this with authority, with Christian love, with compassion, and with irrepressible enthusiasm. He lived not in faith or hope, but in certainty of Christ's Resurrection. This was an enormous joy, but also a responsibility. Christianity for him was simple, in the very best sense: it consisted in "simply" answering Christ's call to "Follow me," in the awareness that one did not follow empty-handed, but carrying one's own cross to Calvary. This is summed up in these final words from Meditations on a Theme, *which encapsulate everything he said and everything he lived by.*

This stirring passage appears in Meditations on a Theme *as if it were by Metropolitan Anthony without acknowledgment that it had been largely copied from a passage by St. Luke of Simferopol.*

The Lord himself has taken upon his shoulder the first cross, the heaviest, most appalling cross, but after him thousands and thousands of men, women, and children have taken upon themselves their own crosses, lesser crosses, but how often these crosses, which are lesser than Christ's, remain so frightening for us. Innumerable crowds of people have lovingly, obediently, walked in the footsteps of Christ, treading the long way, the tragic way shown by our Lord, a way tragic but that leads from this earth to the very throne of God, into the Kingdom of God. They walk, carrying their crosses, they walk now for two thousand years, those who believe in Christ. They walk on, following him, crowd after crowd, and on the way we see crosses, innumerable crosses, on which are crucified the disciples of Christ. Crosses, one cross after the other, and however far we look, it is crosses and crosses again. We see the bodies of the martyrs, we see the heroes of the spirit, we see monks and nuns, we see priests and pastors, but many, many more people do we see, ordinary, simple, humble people of God who have willingly taken upon themselves the cross of Christ. There is no end to this procession. They walk throughout the centuries knowing that Christ has foretold us that they will have sorrow on this earth, but that the Kingdom of God is theirs. They walk with the heavy crosses, rejected, hated, because of truth, because of the name of Christ. They walk, they walk, these pure victims of God, the old and the young, children and grownups. But *where are we?* Are we going to stand and look, to see this long procession, this throng of people with shining eyes, with hope unquenched, with unfaltering love, with incredible joy in their hearts, pass us by? Shall we not join them, this eternally moving crowd, which is marked as a crowd of victims, but also as little children of the Kingdom? Are we not going to take up our cross and follow Christ? Christ has commanded us to follow him. He has invited us to the banquet of his Kingdom and he is at the head of the procession. Nay, he is together with each of those who walk. Is this a nightmare? How can blood and flesh endure this tragedy, the sight of all these martyrs, new and old? Because Christ is Risen, because we do not see in the Lord who walks ahead of us the defeated prophet of Galilee as he was seen by his tormentors, his persecutors. We know him now in the glory of the Resurrection. We know that every word of his is true. We know that the Kingdom of God is ours if we simply follow him.   — *Meditations on a Theme*, 123

Permissions

MODERN SPIRITUAL MASTERS
Robert Ellsberg, Series Editor

Already published:

Dietrich Bonhoeffer (edited by Robert Coles)
Simone Weil (edited by Eric O. Springsted)
Henri Nouwen (edited by Robert A. Jonas)
Pierre Teilhard de Chardin (edited by Ursula King)
Anthony de Mello (edited by William Dych, S.J.)
Charles de Foucauld (edited by Robert Ellsberg)
Oscar Romero (by Marie Dennis, Rennie Golden,
    and Scott Wright)
Eberhard Arnold (edited by Johann Christoph Arnold)
Thomas Merton (edited by Christine M. Bochen)
Thich Nhat Hanh (edited by Robert Ellsberg)
Rufus Jones (edited by Kerry Walters)
Mother Teresa (edited by Jean Maalouf)
Edith Stein (edited by John Sullivan, O.C.D.)
John Main (edited by Laurence Freeman)
Mohandas Gandhi (edited by John Dear)
Mother Maria Skobtsova (introduction by Jim Forest)
Evelyn Underhill (edited by Emilie Griffin)
St. Thérèse of Lisieux (edited by Mary Frohlich)
Flannery O'Connor (edited by Robert Ellsberg)
Clarence Jordan (edited by Joyce Hollyday)
G. K. Chesterton (edited by William Griffin)
Alfred Delp, S.J. (introduction by Thomas Merton)
Bede Griffiths (edited by Thomas Matus)
Karl Rahner (edited by Philip Endean)
Sadhu Sundar Singh (edited by Charles E. Moore)
Pedro Arrupe (edited by Kevin F. Burke, S.J.)
Romano Guardini (edited by Robert A. Krieg)
Albert Schweitzer (edited by James Brabazon)
Caryll Houselander (edited by Wendy M. Wright)
Brother Roger of Taizé (edited by Marcello Fidanzio)